Praise for *Salmon to Siddh*

Don Fergusson's story is an inspiring journey from struggle and resistance to a state of flow and equanimity. His lessons could be touchstones in your awakening as well.
—Deepak Chopra

I love this book as it's a true story of someone who seemingly had it all, realized what he had was worth very little, courageously set about to truly find meaning and purpose in his life, and has succeeded. It's a true love story in that he is now living a life he loves.
—Ron Hulnick, President, University of Santa Monica, co-author of *Loyalty To Your Soul: The Heart of Spiritual Psychology*

Marvelous book! The insights into love and relationships and life priorities are so deep and so helpful. It is rare to find someone who writes from the heart and writes well—Don has a powerful message and a wonderful story to tell.
—Steve McDonald, author of *House of Mirrors*

Salmon to Siddhartha taught me that our value is in being, rather than doing. We can lead a calmer, more fulfilled, and enjoyable life if we recognize the lessons and opportunities that come our way. We can transform great adversity into wisdom.
—Robin Ferracone, CEO, Farient Advisors, author of *Fair Pay, Fair Play: Aligning Executive Performance and Pay*

I like the premise of the book and that it lays out constructive steps that people can take to achieve happiness in their lives. It is also a strong testament that Don was willing to reject the status quo and make the tough decision to chart a different path in regard to his life's work.
—Tom Reed, President & COO, Rust-Oleum Group, RPM International, Inc.

This is a good page-turner where you can't wait to see what happens next. The book is candid, humorous, deep, but always an easy read. I took away practical ideas that will make me a better person, husband, friend, father.
—Robert J. Zollars, Chairman and Member of Governance & Nominating Committee, Vocera Communications, Inc.

This book reflects the wisdom gleaned from a lifetime of striving towards authenticity, excellence, and loyalty to loved ones, while learning the most important lesson of all: being loyal to one's own soul. Don's journey provides valuable lessons to those with ambition and drive, who yearn to live life with a deep sense of fulfillment, peace and power.
—Dr. Noushin Bayat, Leadership Coach and Consultant

I didn't want to put the book down, and I thought about it when I went to sleep. It was just like a good movie.
—Aaron Kessler, manager of Meredith Kessler, Ironman champion

Everyone can relate to the struggling Salmon no matter where they may be on life's journey. Having the 5 Principles to call upon would benefit those facing marital, career-related or even addiction challenges.
—Andy Pitler, Vice-President Sales, Health Integrated, Inc.

I normally take 2 months to read a book, however I finished this book in just two sittings. I am certainly the Salmon, however I will now pull over on the side of the bank and enjoy the calmer waters where possible.
—John Kerr, owner of Stonefly Lodge, New Zealand

Jesus encouraged his disciples to follow an approach similar to the Siddhartha way: Seek His vision for your life, listen to the guidance of the Holy Spirit, trust God in discerning the opportunities that float by, and then step out proactively in faith.
—Kimra Green, Midlothian, VA

I found the book very inspiring and full of deep wisdom and practical knowledge. I am applying the principles to my current life circumstances.
—Virginia Lee, Chico, CA

SALMON TO SIDDHARTHA

5 Vital Principles for an Extraordinary Life

Don Fergusson

SALMON TO SIDDHARTHA

5 Vital Principles for an Extraordinary Life

Learn more at:

donfergusson.com

Watch award-winning music videos and listen to Vanaka's gold-medal winning album of eclectic Indie rock at:

vanakamusic.com

Cover illustration by John Mavroudis

Design by Irene Rietschel

English translation of excerpts from Hermann Hesse's *Siddhartha* by Irene Rietschel with adjustments by Jonathan Brennan and Don Fergusson, from the German text originally published in 1922.

Table of Contents

"When someone is seeking," said Siddhartha,
"it happens easily that his eye only sees the thing he is seeking,
that he is incapable of finding anything, absorbing anything,
because he is only thinking of the thing he is seeking, because he
has a goal, because he is obsessed with this goal.

To be seeking means having a goal. Finding, however, means
being free, standing openly, having no goal. You, venerable one,
may indeed be a seeker, because, striving towards your goal, you
do not see many a thing standing right before your eyes."

—Hermann Hesse, Siddhartha

Preface

I swam and swam until my heart pounded and my breath grew short. In a wide, blue river outside Yosemite, I struggled upstream. After a few minutes, I finally lifted my head, shook the water from my eyes, and realized I hadn't traveled a single foot. The current held me in place. And when I stopped swimming and treaded water, I drifted backwards.

At that time, in my early twenties, on the frontier of my first career and marriage, I approached life as if it were a river rushing toward me. In shallow waters, I could push one foot forward ahead of the other, feeling unsteadily for solid bottom amongst the rocks and pebbles that made my balance precarious. Yet when least expected, my foot found a hole or caught a slippery boulder, and down I went into the icy water, shuddering and gasping for breath. Other times, in the depths, I just swam like hell, fighting my way to goals I'd set upstream, as if they were dry rocks to which I could cling. When I made it to those goals, I seldom granted myself time for a momentary celebration before plunging back in to swim some more—because that's all I knew to do.

I've learned since that when I focus too intently on some predetermined goal, I miss opportunities to make better choices for myself. Often in the past, I failed to examine what was actually driving me up river, whether I was swimming out of obligation, or fear, or love. By trying to *do* more, I observed less. I didn't realize I had a choice of where I applied my energy. I misunderstood that the *goal*, that jagged dry rock, was often less important than what I had to learn through the *process* of achieving the goal, the swim itself.

As we get older, we can more clearly see that how we have negotiated the bends and turns, the rapids and falls of our lives, has brought us exquisitely, precisely, to where we find ourselves. Just as a river's water may be fed by the clouds that gather their moisture from the oceans to which those rivers flow, so too can a higher, cloud-level perspective reveal to us the divine nature of the currents and cycles in our own lives.

That is, if we're open to discovering that divine nature.

I have written this book for those souls who feel as if they are swimming for their lives; for those who may be caught in the swirling eddies of stagnant marriages or who have stumbled into the deep, angry whirlpools of divorce. I hope to inspire courage in those who find themselves endlessly struggling upstream in jobs that no longer bring deep satisfaction, and who are afraid to stop swimming. The book offers guidance for those launching themselves in search of new meaning and happiness in their relationships, careers, and lives, and support for those who sense a yearning in their hearts that pulses like the gentlest current.

Who is Siddhartha?

The fictional title character of the 1922 novel by Hermann Hesse, Siddhartha is a seeker of enlightenment. Born to a noble family, a priestly caste on the highest rung of society, he lives in northern India at the time of Buddha, 500 years before Christ.

In his youth, Siddhartha rejects the elite life, observing that the priests *teach* rituals to attain a blissful state, but never *experience* bliss themselves. Against the wishes of his father, Siddhartha joins a band of thin, nearly naked ascetics who denounce bodily pleasures through fasting and celibacy, with the aim of conquering the Self. He experiences pain, hunger, thirst, and fatigue to extreme degrees; but after three years, Siddhartha realizes neither he nor his fellow pilgrims have found spiritual liberation. When he meets the Buddha in person, Siddhartha recognizes that this man alone has achieved enlightenment. But Siddhartha also realizes that he himself will not experience enlightenment merely by spending time in the Buddha's presence or by following the proclamations of other spiritual masters.

Disillusioned, Siddhartha immerses himself in the material world. He adopts two mentors, a shrewd merchant and a beautiful courtesan, and learns to play the games of money and carnal pleasure. Soon he becomes rich, with a house and servants, wine and women. He experiences gains and losses, joys and sorrows, lust and hate, becoming just like those he once scorned. Addicted to possessions, he grows sick of life.

Siddhartha's awakening comes in his early forties, as he contemplates suicide. Moments from casting himself into the depths of a river, he hears in the flowing water the holy word Om, "Perfection." Suddenly surrendering to the flow of life, and accepting all of his past and present, he recognizes that he had to lose his way in the world to find the path back to himself. By experiencing the totality of life, accepting the Divine perfection in all paths, and learning compassion, Siddhartha gains the Buddha's smile for himself.

Introduction

Early in my life I lived mainly like a salmon, the painful approach: dive like hell into the fast-flowing river, driven by an innate sense of obligation, swim against the current, and fight my way through until I am exhausted. Granted, at that point salmon then have sex, which might make the whole swim worthwhile. But after that they die, or some big bear eats them for breakfast.

I've learned there's another way.

Instead of struggling against the current, what if we sat by the banks of the river like Siddhartha, with a clear intention of the experience we want? And then listened and watched. Paid attention to what floated by. Had faith that the Universe would bring us what we truly want—and, more importantly, offer us what we really *need* for the next step in our learning, growth, and spiritual evolution. We do have to pay attention, of course. We need to be receptive. And when we see something float by that aligns with our intention, we have to reach out, grab it, and do something with it.

So, I'm not saying the Siddhartha Way takes no effort.

That would be like the attitude of the girl I knew my freshman year at college, who decided to stop studying because if Jesus wanted her to fail she would. And she did.

I do believe that reaching goals in life takes conscious effort (after all, Jesus encouraged his disciples to use their own conscious efforts to move forward on their mission). The wise way, however, puts more emphasis on the *conscious* part than the *effort*.

What I've become more conscious about over time is how the goals I set for myself, those destinations I swim upstream towards like a salmon, really just provide the means by which I can learn.

Look at it this way. On the surface, we think that getting from Point A to Point B is what life is all about. Let's imagine the A-to-B journey as a horizontal line that you might think of as the "Goal Road." Point B, the goal, might be finding the perfect job. Making the next sales quota. Earning your first million dollars. Or your next. Buying your own airplane. Finding a mate, getting married, having a kid.

What we encounter along the road to our goals are obstacles that keep us from reaching Point B. After all, if there were no obstacles, we'd already be at Point B, right?

The salmon approach treats life like a raging river flowing against us on our way from Point A to Point B. When we hit an obstacle, like a big boulder, we have to fight our way around it. Or maybe we just keep bashing our noses against that unyielding obstacle, believing it will move.

But the obstacles we encounter can provide a way to gain more consciousness about how we're living life. They provide an opportunity to climb up a "Learning Ladder" that rises above our Goal Road. Consider what could happen if, instead of bashing our noses or exhausting ourselves, we choose to gain a higher perspective and ask, "What do I have to learn from this?" We could gain greater awareness about ourselves, what's driving us, and whether we actually need to swim in this direction right now. With greater consciousness about how we're living life, we might be able to accomplish our goals faster and easier—and save ourselves a lot of hard swimming.

Believe me, I've had plenty of experience as a salmon, and my old conditioning still has me jumping into a river at the first sign of trouble or a challenging goal. But before I get too soaked now, I climb out and sit on the bank to dry off and gain some perspective.

I wonder how my life would have changed had I known all this when I was running myself ragged reorganizing Rust-Oleum Corporation, my family business. I wonder if I would have spent two and a half years in a divorce war. Quite honestly, for that marathon swim through the divorce, I didn't end up better off financially— in fact, much worse, from extended legal and consulting bills. I didn't gain a better custody arrangement, and all the animosity only created more stress on my children and less cooperation between myself and my ex-wife.

I might have chosen differently if I knew better then, but I've learned not to judge the past. Everything happens for our learning, growth, and spiritual evolution, to help us gain more consciousness about how we're living life. We take a big step in our spiritual evolution and consciousness when we realize that the ultimate goal of life is to gain wisdom about how to accept and love ourselves and others unconditionally (while learning to establish self-honoring conditions and boundaries for the relationships we're in).

In this book, I have related my story to that of Siddhartha, who embarked on a powerful human journey of intense failure and hard-won wisdom. He developed his philosophy by experiencing numerous extremes, finally realizing that happiness would not arrive on a silver platter but requires definitive action and deepened self-awareness. By drawing an analogy between the story of Siddhartha and my own, I am suggesting that my journey mirrors a universal human journey. The struggle through despair and difficulty towards spiritual enlightenment yields powerful lessons for us all.

My life experiences provided lots of opportunity for learning, but surprisingly, it was my mid-life decision to become a musician that helped me crystallize the 5 vital principles for living with greater awareness and creating more of what I want. I call these the *Siddhartha Principles*. In summary, these principles are:

1. **ACCEPT.** Meet yourself where you are, without judgment.

2. **LEARN.** Find the lesson in your present challenge.

3. **CLARIFY.** Create an Ideal Scene of your desired experience.

4. **ACT.** Take small steps every day to create your desired experience.

5. **TRUST.** Have faith that your life is unfolding perfectly.

The value of these principles became clear as I embraced a seemingly impossible one-year project: taking up bass guitar in my fifties, forming a rock band called The Ride with my wife Stacey, learning to play an hour-long set of classic rock tunes, writing an original song to record at London's Abbey Road Studios and playing a gig at The Cavern Club in Liverpool, just as the Beatles did. I learned more than just how to play music through this rock and roll ride. Accordingly, I've named the chapters for many of the song titles of the original Cavern Club set because, serendipitously, they mirror my life's story and the lessons learned along the way.

This he had learned by the river, this one thing:
to wait, to be patient, to listen.

—Hermann Hesse, *Siddhartha*

[All quotes are from *Siddhartha*, unless otherwise noted.]

Chapter 1: All Shook Up

Joy jumped in his father's heart for the son, who was quick
to learn, thirsty for knowledge; he saw growing in him a great
sage and priest, a prince among the Brahmans...This was how
everybody loved Siddhartha. He brought joy to all; he delighted
all. However, Siddhartha did not bring joy to himself, he was
no delight to himself...loved by all, everybody's joy, he still did
not carry joy in his heart...Siddhartha had begun to nurture
discontent in himself...his mind was not satisfied, his soul was
not calm, his heart was not appeased.

From the outside looking in, by the age of 37 I had the perfect
life. President of a recognized company, I was married with two
wonderful little children, living in a beautiful house on a lake in
the northern suburbs of Chicago. All my ducks in a row. Set for life.

But, in the hour before dawn on a Friday the 13th in July, I
awoke feeling troubled, still uneasy from the conversation I'd had
with my wife Sally the previous night. I'd been aware for several
months that not all was well with my marriage of 13 years. We'd
had no real fights or arguments, but there was a distance between
us. We didn't spend much time together, and our conversations
were mainly limited to our schedules, to-do lists and activities for
the children.

I'd taken a recent fishing trip on a remote lake in Manitoba
with my best friend Tim, and as we cast our lines from the boat, I
confided that something seemed out of kilter in my marriage with
Sally.

"Hmm," Tim said, busy reeling in a pike.

Tim had been one of my closest buddies since our fraternity days together in college. He married his college sweetheart. Since they lived in Chicago, my wife and I spent a lot of fun times with them. That is, until their marriage abruptly ended.

I introduced Tim to a therapist, Henry Wickersham, to help him through his divorce. And I spent lots of time consoling my best friend: I invited Tim to stay at our suburban home a weekend or two a month. I took him on a New Year's Eve trip along with my wife and two other couples in our close group of friends, and a couple months later, we went windsurfing together. I felt sorry for him that his marriage was ending so painfully.

When I returned from Manitoba, I asked Sally to go to counseling with me. "You know, I've been so worried about Tim," I said, "but I don't think we're doing so well, either. Maybe we should get some counseling to figure out our problems, so we don't end up like him."

I was surprised that my wife rejected the idea. "Go get some counseling for yourself if you want," she said. "I don't have any interest in joining you."

I didn't know what to say, so I just mumbled, "I love you."

Her reply, with a sweet smile and sad brown eyes, didn't set me at ease: "I know you do."

I decided to visit Tim's therapist myself. When I'd called Henry Wickersham the previous day to make an appointment, I explained, "Henry, I think I'm having some problems in my marriage and would like to talk with you about it. I'm going to ask my wife to join me, too."

"Sure," he said. "Come on in. Even if your wife doesn't want to."

On the way to his office, I wondered how he knew Sally didn't want to join us, but I figured maybe he'd been down this path before.

In a not-too-comfortable armchair in Henry's modest office, I made the case for myself:

"I've tried to balance my work with my home life. Early in our marriage, we had a flare-up over my work hours, and I learned not to bring paperwork home on the weekends. I try to minimize my business travel. And every night I'm home, I give the children a bath, read them a story, sing them a song, and put them to bed. Until recently, Sally and I had dinner out together once a week. And I've made it a priority for the two of us to take a vacation together every couple of months. I don't understand why lately she seems so distant." My voice cracked and my eyes welled with tears. "How do I get her to tell me what the problem is?"

Long silence. Henry drew a slow breath, as if to measure his words. "You know, Don," he said in a quiet voice, "this might be more serious than you realize. I suggest you talk with Sally soon. It might be closer to the ninth inning than you think."

Ninth inning? I was dumbfounded. I thought I was just throwing the opening pitch! With furrowed brow, I nodded. End of meeting. I wrote him a check for a hundred-and-twenty-dollars, thank you very much.

The next evening, after tucking our children into bed, I caught up with Sally in the kitchen. "So, Sally, can we talk? I saw Henry Wickersham yesterday afternoon, and I want to tell you what he said."

With a sigh and sad eyes, Sally agreed. She led me down the long hallway, across the foyer, through double French doors into the formal living room. I'd always found the room cold and uninviting, and I could count on one hand the number of times I'd sat in this room in the five years we'd lived there.

I sat down next to Sally. The look in her eyes told me she had something to say. She took my hand in hers, cast her brown eyes downward, pursed her lips, then fixed her gaze on me.

"Don, I've thought a lot about what you said the other night, about whether I could make a commitment to work with you in counseling. I've decided I can't, and that I want a divorce. I know you love me, but the love I once had inside for you isn't there anymore."

What? My brain whirled. I couldn't believe what I was hearing.

"What do you mean *divorce?* What about our children, this house, our *life?*" I felt like the lead player in a surreal movie, fighting to maintain my sanity. "How can you have your mind made up when we haven't even talked? Just tell me what the problem is, and I'll fix it."

She told me she'd been unhappy with our marriage for a long time.

In the hour that followed, I tried in vain to pry out the reason she wanted a divorce. I got angry, I coddled, I cried, I implored. "I just don't love you anymore," became her refrain. No details. Then, in a flash of intuition, I asked, "Are you in love with somebody else?"

She cast her eyes downward. "Yes," she replied. "But I won't tell you who it is. If you really want to find out, I suppose you could." Sally sat quietly on her sofa.

My brain exploded. My heart raced. I was furious. I had to get out of there. Shaking, I stumbled down the hallway to the garage, climbed into my car, floored it out of the garage and down the driveway, then sped down a dark two-lane highway. I had no destination. I dialed Tim. It was midnight.

"Hey, sorry if I woke you. You're not going to believe what's coming down here tonight," I blurted out, my breath short, my heart pounding, my stomach knotted. "Sally tells me she wants a divorce, she's in love with somebody else, and she won't tell me who. Do you have any idea who it might be?"

"Uh, hang on," Tim said. "I have to get my glasses."

Huh?

My mind raced, flooded with memories and sudden realizations. Sally working late hours at a needlework shop in Chicago near Tim's home. Tim and I off to a wine tasting in the city dressed in matching tuxedos, and Sally sending us off with the words, "I'm not sure I should trust my men going off looking so good." Sally re-arranging our seating with friends at a recent rock concert to put me on the far side of another couple, so she could sit next to Tim. Tim not signing the check he gave me to pay for the recent fishing trip. Sally and Tim spending hours chatting and laughing in the backyard hammock after we returned from the fishing trip, when Sally would hardly greet me hello. At the time I thought, *Good. Maybe Tim will find out what's going on with Sally and he'll be able to help me.*

By the time he came back to the phone, I had a sinking feeling as a terrible thought crossed my mind. "Tim, you're going to think this is crazy for me to say, and I hope you'll forgive me," I said hesitantly. "Tell me it isn't you."

Long silence.

"Don, we have to talk," Tim stammered.

"What do you mean we have to talk?" I said incredulously.

"I don't know what I can say or do," he said.

I threw down the phone. I did a one-eighty as I hit the brakes, spun the wheel, and punched the gas. I fishtailed in a streak toward home, skidding through the stop signs, racing to escape this reality.

When I stepped into the back hallway, I yelled at the top of my voice, "Where are you?" and found Sally sitting unmoved in her living room. I screamed, "Well, I just had an interesting phone call with my friend Tim. Why didn't you tell me it was him?"

Sally just looked at me, not saying a word. My head exploded. I lunged forward, screaming, "How could you do this to me?" Sally fled down the hall, out the door and sped off in her car.

My God, I thought, *I'm losing my wife, my family, my life. What will I have left? What do I tell my children? How will I survive the fishbowl of Rust-Oleum? What will all those people think of me?*

As I awoke for work on Monday morning, dreading the news I had to tell my staff, a waking nightmare shook me. I imagined Tim moving into my house, with my children, on my money. I had no idea how long I'd been in the dark about their affair. That morning, during my phone call to Henry Wickersham, the marriage counselor, he confided that Tim had come into his office with a woman several months earlier to get advice about their affair and how to tell her husband. The woman was Sally. Henry was shocked when he realized she was my wife. It was already the Eighth Inning by then, so now I understood why he declared it was nearly the Ninth by the time I went to see him.

I wouldn't learn my first life lesson from this ordeal until years later, but here it is now: *Sometimes we have to go into the very darkest depths before we can surface into the light. And often, what we deem as the worst crisis of our lives turns out to be the biggest blessing.*

Chapter 2: In My Life

Wind back the clock. I'd been president of my family company, Rust-Oleum, for five years, having taken the helm at the ripe old age of 32. Counting summer jobs there throughout high school, college, and graduate business school, I already had 21 years with the company under my belt—not to mention growing up watching my father work there.

The work hadn't been easy. I'd been launched into the company full time right out of graduate school when my dad died of a heart attack at 54. He'd been president since his older brother, my uncle, died of a heart attack at 46; and my uncle had become president when their father, my grandfather and the inventor and founder of Rust-Oleum, died of a heart attack at 63.

Ever see the Tom Hanks film *Forrest Gump*? Remember the character Lieutenant Dan, whose forefathers all died in battle beginning with the Revolutionary War and continuing through the Civil War, World War I, and World War II? Dan thought it was his duty to die in battle, too, this time in Vietnam, and he was really bummed out that all he managed to do was get his legs blown off.

Well, I had kind of a Lieutenant Dan thing going.

My grandfather was a legend larger than life. Near the turn of the 20th century, he left Scotland at the age of 15, involuntarily. One of nine children, he was bonded by his parents to the captain of a sailing ship crossing the Atlantic.

Over the next 40 years, Robert Fergusson rose from cabin boy to captain himself, taking command of sailing ships and steamers between the U.S., Europe, Asia, and up and down the Mississippi.

His exploits at sea remain legendary. He once captained a merchant vessel sailing the Yangtze River to Nanking, China, to pick up cargo for delivery to Hong Kong. Along the way, river pirates attacked his boat. As the Chinese junks pulled alongside, his stomach tightened and his mind raced—he was badly outnumbered. Quickly, he attached a hose to the ship's boiler. As each pirate poked his head above deck, the Captain seared them with a blast of steam, while the first mate smacked them over the head with a belaying pin. One by one, the pirates plunked back into the muddy waters of the Yangtzee, and the Captain resumed his journey.

Most famously, an account in the New York World-Telegram newspaper described an incident that portrayed the Captain's integrity, grit, and impulsive generosity. In October 1916, he joined a crew of 16 men as second officer on a small steamship, the Vigilant, sailing for England from St. John, Newfoundland. Within three days, the skies turned black, churning with gale force winds and driving rain. The sea rose like a range of dark mountains, huge waves crashing over the deck. With each new swell and pounding, it seemed the top-heavy boat must capsize. Still many miles off the Irish coast and edging toward nightfall, the captain of the ship cried, "We've done all we can. We've got to abandon her!" He wired an SOS. After what seemed an eternity, a passing liner, the Ryndam, pulled alongside and lowered a lifeboat. But Fergusson wasn't leaving. Clinging to a rail to keep from washing overboard, he declared, "I was hired to bring this ship to port, and I won't abandon her." The boat's captain, incredulous, called him a fool. Without looking back, the captain and a dozen crewmen scampered onto the rescue ship. One Irishman hesitated, then turned back to look the Scotsman in the eye. "Okay, Scotty," he laughed. "It's crazy, but I'll have a go at it." Moments later the Yankee fireman growled, "All right, all right. I'll fire your damned tub for you."

The Ryndam steamed away, and Fergusson lashed himself to the wheel to keep from being washed overboard by the relentless avalanche of water. The night brought horror, the bow buried beneath every breaker, the 226-ton ship straining to rise after each blow. All through the next day, the storm and sea battered the ship, shoving it off course. The men could get no food, no water. One at the helm, two down below, fighting for their lives. When night came again, the steering gear jammed. They couldn't hold the ship steady. Suddenly she swung, and the seas began to drag her down. A big wave slammed the *Vigilant* on the starboard side. Deck lashings snapped, the anchor broke loose, and in the engine room, the dynamo shaft snapped, and the lights went out. The *Vigilant* heeled over and didn't come back, hanging, canted, about to capsize. Just then another great wave struck her port side, slamming the ship back upright. She wobbled forward, driving into the next wave.

All night, they worked on the steering gear. At dawn, the sea subsided and the helm came back into service. Soon after, to Fergusson's surprise and relief, a patrol ship appeared, an officer calling to them through a megaphone, signaling that he'd guide them in. The *Vigilant* kept pace until nightfall, when they had to douse the lights—sailing through the war zone—and Fergusson kept losing sight of the ship, straining to see through the darkness. Finally, after 50 hours without sleep, food, or water, the men brought the battered ship to dock in Castletownbere, Ireland.

The town received them as heroes, and the mayor honored the men with a formal celebration and luncheon, including all the notables of the community. When the festivities ended, the three shipmates headed back to the dock, followed at a respectful distance by a group of young boys. Fergusson noticed that all were without shoes and socks, despite the chill of that late autumn day. Like the Pied Piper, he steered the entire entourage into a shoe store, demanding the proprietor fit them all with shoes and stockings— and charge it to the mayor.

The qualities of courage, integrity, perseverance, and empathy demonstrated by the Captain certainly raised the ante for what I believed was expected of me—and what I expected of myself.

⤳

As a child, I was aware that my grandfather had been married once before, that my dad and my uncle were his second family.

My parents didn't talk about it, knew few details, had no interest in tracking down the story. It wouldn't be until years later, when I did a genealogy study as part of a psychology masters degree, that I learned the Captain's first marriage ended when he discovered his wife was having an affair with his first mate. Interestingly, the purpose of the study was to reflect on what behavioral and emotional patterns may have shown up in our own lives, transcending from past generations. Well, well.

The story would become eerie foreshadowing for my own situation. It also serves as a lesson about what I'd eventually discover as *Siddhartha Principle* 5: **TRUST. Have faith that your life is unfolding perfectly.** Had the Captain's first mate not betrayed him, he wouldn't have married my grandmother, had my father, and I wouldn't be here.

Fortunately for me and for Rust-Oleum, the Captain survived his divorce and his adventures at sea. And his legend continued. So did his personal reinvention, as he went from ship's captain to inventor to businessman.

During his many years at sea, he noticed that fish oil could prevent rust. When spilled on the iron decks, the oil soaked through the rust, driving out the air and moisture that caused it, preventing further corrosion. Raw fish oil made a great rust-preventive coating, except for two problems: It never dried, and it smelled like fish.

Then, as now, there was not much of a market for a fish-scented paint.

Undaunted, Captain Fergusson became fascinated with the idea of creating a fish-oil-based coating. While in charge of a laid-up fleet of World War I vessels at Nine Mile Point on the Mississippi River above New Orleans, he cooked fish oil on the galley stoves and slapped his experiments on the rusting ships. Eventually, he found a combination of heat and additives that worked. In 1921, he founded the paint company that would become Rust-Oleum, selling cans of his brew from the trunk of his Model T Ford. He'd drive around looking for rusting industrial fences, surreptitiously paint them with his fish oil formula, return weeks later to surprise the owners with the results—and make the sale.

The valiant Scotsman spent the last 19 years of his life trying to launch the business. He went broke twice, and after the ravaging Great Depression of the 1930s, his annual sales had plummeted by one-half, to less than a hundred thousand dollars. On October 13, 1940, during a business trip, he collapsed dead of a heart attack on a train platform in Toronto, Canada.

His sons, my father Donald and his brother Bob, took over the business at the ages of 18 and 20, respectively. Though most of the staff quit, quite certain the company would turn belly up, the brothers persevered, mortgaging everything they owned. Bob got drafted into World War II, their mother died, and then my dad got drafted, too. My mother and the remaining employees kept the operation going. When the brothers returned, they pushed Rust-Oleum forward, riding the post-war boom. Manufacturing expanded and the sales force grew. Leveraging a national base of industrial distributors, they entered the consumer market in the early 1960s with small-sized cans and one of the first paints in aerosols. Finally, the business gained some traction.

Then in 1966 my uncle Bob suddenly died. My dad took over the company for the last 10 years of his own life, through a nervous breakdown, diverticulitis, an irregular heartbeat, angioplasty, and a pacemaker. He struggled to create a management team that could survive him. But it seemed he could never sit back, never rest. Every time he'd get a team in place, some major problem would arise, and back into the raging current he'd plunge. I witnessed him in fully stressed-out action when I worked as a trainee in field sales one summer during college, when he fired the vice-president of sales, the vice-president of marketing, the director of marketing, and the personnel director all in the same day.

My dad took two vacations a year, and those were the only times I saw him relax. Otherwise, he put in long days at the office, then took paperwork home at night. He volunteered for charity work and served as president of Rotary and the local school board. On weekends, he shifted from mental work to physical work. Though he bought a 120-acre farm in northern Illinois as a weekend sanctuary, he always had a project going, and usually roped me into it: removing miles of barbed-wire fences, installing miles of wood fences, painting miles of wood fences, tearing down a dairy barn, building a horse barn, building a five-acre lake, lining the perimeter of the five-acre lake with thirty-pound chunks of concrete broken from the foundation of the old dairy barn to keep muskrats from digging through the dike.

Guess who got elected as the concrete chunk placer during one hot August summer? As the temperature rose over 90 degrees to compete with the humidity, I lifted those heavy, rough concrete blocks off a pile, one-by-one, then lugged them to the lakeshore. Just as I reached the bottom of the pile, here came my dad on the tractor, dumping another load from the bucket. My hay fever kicked in so badly, I ran out of tissues and blew my nose into my T-shirt until it was soaked. Hot, sneezing, eyes itching, nose running, arms aching, sweat pouring—and here's another stack. Gee, so nice we built this lake and stocked it with bass so we could have fun on the weekends. I felt like I'd drawn prison detail, and the warden didn't care if I was dying.

I was a Salmon in training.

I worked hard in high school, graduating twenty-first in my class of over 1,000. Knowing my destiny, I earned an undergraduate business degree at the College of William & Mary in Virginia, even though I preferred English literature and art history. I served as captain of the gymnastics team for all four years, despite knocking my front teeth through my lip after landing a double back-flip off the high bar onto my face, and then cracking my head open and breaking my nose on the high bar itself in the process of learning a new dismount.

As I look back now from a point of greater awareness, I realize I was driven by a deep subconscious feeling that I really wasn't good enough. I had to prove myself. I had to live up to the unstated expectations of my family. Obligation outweighed fun. As I began to leave my childhood behind, I felt the looming weight of the responsibilities that lay ahead. And I sensed that to carry them, I would need to abandon much of who I was. God forbid I should show any weakness, sadness, or vulnerability, exposing a character flaw. Perhaps even at that tender age, I formed an irrational belief that unless I accomplished all that was expected of me—all that I expected of myself—I wouldn't be loveable.

My summer jobs at Rust-Oleum, which began at the age of 16, weren't much of an improvement over the work detail at the farm. My dad started me off in the hottest, heaviest, dirtiest jobs in the paint factory, loading paint mills with hundreds of fifty-pound bags of pigment alongside a burly ex-Marine, our crew leader, who had just returned from the Vietnam War. At the beginning of each summer, I'd do my best to hide my true identity, with the hopes of striking up a friendship before my workmates discovered I was the dreaded son of the boss. It wouldn't last long. Then everybody would treat me kindly, some would smile in my face but make derogatory remarks behind my back, and any mistake I made was magnified.

Once in that first summer, one of my fellow employees asked for my help. I knew him only as Marty, a recent graduate from my high school, from the other side of town. As I walked by, he was pouring an additive from a 55-gallon drum into a 5-gallon bucket, and dumping the bucket's contents through a hatch to the mixing cylinder on the floor below.

"Hey, Don," he called, "can you pour five more in here? I gotta go to the can."

"Sure," I replied, and began measuring out five more buckets, one at a time, to add to the mix. When he returned, he asked, "How did it go?"

"Fine," I said. "But I ran out of this stuff in the drum. Is there some more of it around?"

"*What?*" he replied, incredulously. "This fifty-five gallon drum was almost half full."

"Well, I poured about four buckets in, but ran short for the last one," I explained.

"Shit!" he screamed. "I meant for you to put in five more *gallons*, not five more buckets!" And with that, he ran down the stairs to find the mixing tank nearly brimming. Fortunately, our crack chemists figured out how to extend the batch, we transferred it to a bigger tank, and our customer agreed to accept a larger shipment. I wish I could say it was simply a brilliant sales technique on my part.

Another mishap that summer couldn't be so easily covered. I'd walked up to the staging area of a large batch of paint, where hundreds of pigment bags lay stacked next to a chute, which connected to the huge cylindrical mixing tank on the floor below. Once loaded with pigment, resin, and additives, the mixing cylinder would be switched on and begin rotating, for hours, to combine the ingredients to the proper viscosity. At this particular moment, I was bored and looking for something to do. Our crew leader walked swiftly past me on his way to measure out another batch. I called after him, "Hey, is this one ready to go?" hoping I could busy myself with the loading. "Yeah," he called back. And I began cutting open fifty-pound bags of yellow pigment, dumping them down the chute to the invisible tank below. Within moments, the plant superintendent barreled up the steep metal stairs from the lower floor—totally covered from head to toe in yellow pigment, like the Pig-Pen character in the *Peanuts* cartoon, a plume of fine yellow dust trailing him up the stairs.

"Who the *hell* is dumping pigment down the chute?" he blustered in anger, spitting, and wiping his glasses. When he returned the spectacles to his yellow-frosted face, he looked up to see the *son of the boss from hell*. The mill below still spun with the *previous* batch. My Marine sergeant crew leader had only meant that the batch had been *measured out*, not ready to be loaded. I'd dumped 100 pounds of pigment on a rolling mill, casting clouds of fine, sticky dust over the entire department, including my crew leader's boss.

"Oh, Donnie, it's you," he stammered, catching his breath and trying to regain his composure. "Well, accidents happen." He smiled thinly, shook his head, and went back downstairs to clean up the mess.

If I'd been anyone else, I'd have been fired. Or strangled. As it was, I think he blamed my crew leader, who was no longer so happy to have me on his crew.

My, working in this fishbowl is fun, I thought to myself sarcastically. *And this is just the beginning of my long career.* I shivered with dread at the thought.

It would take more than 30 years for me to discover how resentful my "inner teen" felt about having to abandon the things I loved in order to take on the obligations of the family business. Much to my astonishment, I would realize in my 50s that the younger part of me remained hard-wired deep within.

That part of me, still 18 at heart, loved rock music, played a set of blue-sparkle Ludwig drums along with my Beatles albums, enjoyed art and literature, and found peace in fishing and nature.

As I saw myself taking boring business classes, donning the suit that would be my daily uniform for 17 years, leaving behind the things that made my heart sing for the sake of obligation, my "inner teen" felt betrayed. Without the tools or experience to integrate those two parts of myself, not knowing I could still allow me to "be me" despite my outer circumstances, I buried my "inner teen."

He tried to make a reappearance when, after my first year at Northwestern University's Kellogg Graduate School of Management, I decided I didn't want the *son of the boss* gig. *Maybe,* I thought to myself, *I should just try to get a job as a marketing manager for Browning Sporting Goods in Utah, hunt and fish a lot, and think about coming back to Rust-Oleum later.*

My dad and the Universe had a different agenda.

Sandwiched between my two years at Kellogg, the summer marked my first life crisis, my transition from youth to adulthood. To send me on my way, I received two serendipitous parting gifts from my dad, one in the form of his time, the other in words.

Since the year I turned thirteen, I'd been going on two-week fishing trips each summer with my dad. And from the very first trip, we'd established a comfortable pattern. I'd invite a friend, and my dad would bring my mother's father. My friend and I fished in our own separate boat, motoring off each day on our own adventures, while my dad and "Pop-Pop" found their own quiet bays. But this summer, my friend cancelled out on our trip to Manitoba at the last minute, and Pop-Pop, nearing 80, confessed he'd gotten too old for the trek. For the first time in 10 years, it would be just my dad and me.

The thought of spending all day in a boat with my dad for two weeks daunted me. I loved him, I held him in the greatest respect, and I also lived in awe of him. He was the consummate "doer." And he often told *me* what to do, or did it for me, which rankled me a bit as a young adult looking to carve my own identity in the world, living in his shadow. We hadn't had many intimate conversations. What would it be like to hang out, just the two of us?

Well, we never caught so many fish as we did that week. As usual, most of them were small, weighing a couple of pounds. Only once in seven years on Lake St. George had I caught a "big one," and even then, at 10 pounds, it was half the size of a trophy. I'd returned that fish to the lake with hopes it would grow bigger and expand the gene pool. Every year, I continued my search for the Monster Pike that surely lay just below my next cast.

Mid-week on a quiet, sunlit western bay, my dad cast to the edge of submerged cabbage weeds, cranked his reel a few times, and felt a solid tug. The hard, steady, confident pull of the fish's first run telegraphed lunker status, a big one. But we'd been fooled before by smaller fish that simply snagged weeds around the line for added weight and pull. Spurning modern technology, my dad used an old bait fishing reel he'd employed for decades. No drag on that reel, which meant that when a big fish yanked hard or took a run, my dad had to crank the reel backwards to give the fish line, so as not to break it. At the same time, he couldn't unwind too fast, fearing a "backlash," in which the Dacron string snarled back on itself to create a knot that could snap the line.

On the third run, the angry fish, resting a moment, allowed itself to be brought close to the boat. No weeds fouled the line. Floating slowly up from a murky four feet to within inches of the surface came the full yard-long length and solid girth of a barracuda-like body. The Monster Pike. *Holy shit!* It easily topped 18 pounds, qualifying for Canada's coveted "Master Angler" award. This one seemed to smile through its sharp white teeth. From the very thinnest sliver of skin on its bony lip hung one, tiny rusted hook of the ancient gray "Lazy Ike" wooden lure. The hook bent precariously against the weight of the fish. With a hard flap of its tail, the Monster dove straight down under the boat, an experienced trick to sever the line on the keel or the dangling prop of the outboard motor. With not an instant of hesitation, my dad plunged the rod tip down into the water, back-reeling as fast as he could while still holding tension on the fish.

Run after run, for 15 minutes, my dad played the Monster as if by aikido, using the energy of the fish against itself, wearing it down. Finally, incredulously, the fish floated up next to the boat, turning exhausted on its side, showing its white underbelly like the flag of surrender. Using the old net provided with our boat, I deftly scooped the fish from the water. As I hoisted the beast toward the boat, the rotted strands burst from the weight and the fish plopped with a splash back into the water, the frail hook broken from its lip. My mouth gaped open in disbelief. So did the fish's. It lay there for an instant looking up at us. Then, with a swish of its tail, it dove down and was gone.

"Goddammit!" I screamed, and threw down the net, then threw down my fishing hat in disgust. I let out a blue streak of profanity that only a well-versed college student could muster, something I'd never done in the presence of my dad.

He just laughed like the Happy Buddha.

There was a good lesson in all that. What a different experience the two of us had, simply by choosing a different response.

Late in the week, as we drifted and cast, I shared my concern that maybe I wasn't good enough to run Rust-Oleum. That's when he gave me the gift of his words, which I didn't heed for years, but have never forgotten.

"Don," he said, "I don't have any doubt in your ability to do it." Then, after a pause, he added, "And if you don't want to, if you just want to run a fishing lodge in Canada, that's fine with me. There's no obligation. You need to decide what makes you happy." After that, we just drifted and cast, in a very long silence.

On our last day of fishing, my dad caught a second Monster, this time a walleye, the biggest we'd ever seen in that lake. We hurried back to the lodge to weigh it. The scale tipped three ounces short of a Master Angler Award at just under eight pounds. The lodge owner looked at my dad with a twinkle in his eye, and joked, "You know, if we were to slip a little lead weight down its throat, like he'd swallowed your hook, you'd be in the record book for this one." My dad just smiled and shook his head. He took the fish back down to the lake, swished it back and forth in the water until it revived, and let it swim away.

By his actions more than his words, my dad taught me something about integrity. Though years later I would veer from being at one with my values, the internal compass he gave me would eventually find true north.

So, my dad nearly caught two award-winning fish in one trip. One more award awaited him. When we returned home, I began my summer job at Rust-Oleum, and my dad went to Springfield, Illinois, for the State Fair horse show. He loved showing Tijuana Brass, a steam-engine of a harness pony, which my dad drove braced in a four-wheeled cart behind the horse, hanging on for dear life. They made it to the championship round. As they lined up alongside the other competitors, waiting for the judges' decision, my dad keeled over and fell from the cart. His heart had stopped. He died before hearing he'd won the blue ribbon.

And so, the baton passed to me as the only family member in a position to run the company. Knowing only the Salmon Way, I jumped headfirst into the raging river, wondering if my own heart attack lay somewhere ahead on the day planner.

I'm not complaining. Working in a family business with a great product and a well-known brand name, having all the opportunities for learning, earning an excellent income—I recognize these as rare gifts that I didn't take for granted. I also appreciated the support I received from my mentor, Rex Reade, appointed as president by my dad a year before he died. Decades earlier, Rex had come to the company from the former "Big Eight" accounting firm Arthur Andersen, rising to head Rust-Oleum's finance department. When my dad's health began to fail, he took the role of Chairman, appointing Rex as President, placing day-to-day operations in Rex's capable hands. Following my dad's death, Rex thought of himself as a steward for the family company, manning the helm only as long as it took for the next Fergusson to take over. Indeed, Rex became a surrogate father to me. As I neared graduation from Kellogg, I'd told him of my plan to gain experience elsewhere before coming to Rust-Oleum. He looked me in the eye and said gravely, "Don, we need you here. You're the only family member who can carry on." And to his credit, after one year, he pulled me out of what was going to be a multi-year stint as a "management trainee," and gave me the extraordinary responsibility of developing a planning process, re-organizing the sales division, and launching a marketing division.

When I stepped full time into the company at age 24, it didn't seem to me that it ran the way they said it should at Kellogg Graduate School of Management. We had no strategic long range plan, no real concept of planning besides budgeting, no marketing division, and few executives who knew the difference between sales and marketing. We had little knowledge of our end customers or where our profits or losses really came from.

We used the latest technology in paint production; however some areas of the company still needed updating. In fact, the first person hired by my grandfather, Anne Kirkland, still hand-signed every executive payroll check.

During my first winter at the company, just out of grad school, the phone on my desk rang at 8:15 a.m. Mrs. Kirkland (as everyone called her) implored me to come pick her up after a storm had dumped three feet of snow in her driveway. Even as heir-apparent, I abandoned the work on my desk and jumped in the car, slipping and sliding across town to save her. The checks had to be signed!

Our strong brand name had carried us far, but in those early years, I had the sense of being on a battleship cruising along at full speed on autopilot in the fog, me shivering on the bridge, not knowing when the shoals or the next torpedo might hit. Of course, I had a logical response. As the third generation and only family member directly involved in the business, I assumed the official role of Martyr, sans white robes and holy water, never mind age and experience.

As my first step, I developed a strategic planning process and helped create a long-term plan. Then I took responsibility for reorganizing a $20 million division that was losing money. I brought in marketing consultants, including Kellogg gurus Phil Kotler and Lou Stern, launched a marketing department for the company, and reorganized the sales division. In the process, I retired our vice president of sales, replaced six of seven regional sales directors, and let go of one-third of the sales force. I narrowed thirteen direct reports into five, then faced the task of cutting our corporate staff by 20 percent so we could actually make some money.

During this period I worked about 60 hours a week, traveled a third of my time, and seldom got more than six hours sleep each night. The only quiet time I had each day at work came before eight in the morning or after six in the evening, and the rest of the day brought constant meetings and the next fire-fight. At one point, a friend of mine asked me if I was having fun. I remember giving him a quizzical look. Fun didn't show up in my job description. Swim on.

Several years into the re-organization process, I had dinner one evening with consultant Phil Kotler, author of the textbook most used in introductory marketing courses across the country. I explained what I saw as our challenges and outlined my plans for re-organization. After a pause, he looked up at me and asked, "How old are you?"

"Twenty-eight, going on forty," I smiled.

I did appreciate the amazing opportunity I had at a very young age to assume heavy responsibilities, and I did have a lot of excellent support in Rex Reade, our Executive Vice-President Bud Bartelt, and many others in our company. But I worked more out of fear and obligation than from love and joy. I figured my destiny just meant fighting like hell upstream until the day I floated belly up.

At the time, I didn't realize that the *situation* didn't cause the stress, but the way I dealt with it. Feeling the weight of responsibility, I ignored my *response-ability*. Regardless of the external circumstances, I had the theoretical *ability* to respond with acceptance, good humor, and inner peace, but I failed to choose this response. Salmon don't have much self-awareness. They just swim.

Despite my success in reorganizing the company and becoming President, I still felt empty inside. One evening at home after work, I stepped out onto the dock alone as the sun set over the lake that lapped my backyard. As I watched the orange glow turn to gray on the water, I sensed a deep unhappiness. Guilt added heaviness to my heart, weighed down with the thought I should just feel more grateful. *Is this all there is?* I wondered. *Is this what I do for the rest of my life, work from dawn to dusk? How could this ever change?*

Five long years later, I still wondered the same thing. But now I had an unexpected answer to how my life might change—with the betrayal by my best friend, the implosion of my marriage, and a long, dark road ahead to resurrection.

Chapter 3: I Should Have Known Better

That fear, that terrible, oppressive fear he felt during the game
of dice, during the agony over the high stakes—he loved that
fear and he continually sought to renew it, to increase it, to
escalate it, because only in this fear did he still feel some kind of
happiness, some kind of excitement, some heightened form of life
in the midst of his satiated, tepid, dull existence.

As the divorce ground on, Sally moved into our basement guest room, while I occupied our upstairs master bedroom. She ignored my demand to move out, I wouldn't leave for fear of giving up the rights to the house and the children, and I refused to concede "irreconcilable differences." Without other grounds for divorce, we faced a mandatory two-year waiting period. My strategy was to create an excruciatingly long and miserable siege, to wear Sally and Tim down.

Yeah, I should have known better.

Swim, salmon, swim.

Looking back, I realize now that this approach escalated our battle. Stuck in rage, I failed to see the sense of humor in the Universe: I'd been given exactly what I really needed, a way out of the relationship. It would be a long time before I grasped *Siddhartha Principle Two* and found the lesson in my present challenge. *Siddhartha Principle Three*, "Clarify your desired experience" was nowhere in sight.

Instead, I waged the battle in many ways. I filed for reconciliation, just to frustrate Sally by stalling the whole process. I cancelled the credit cards and bank accounts, froze our assets. I even sued Tim under an arcane law preventing the crime known as "Alienation of Affection."

The inner battles were even harder. A friend suggested I get some help from a therapist. Light bulbs went off in my head each time I worked with him. The end of my marriage became the beginning of my path to self-awareness and personal growth.

But it was a long path. First I had to get away. Far away. I flew to Australia for 16 days by myself. That was the longest time I'd ever been with myself, and the farthest I'd ever gone from home. I left one little wrapped gift for each of my children for every day I'd be gone, so they could count down to my return.

Arriving in Sydney, I was desperately lonely. After two days, I escaped to the most remote location possible: The Outback. Starting in the small town of Alice Springs, I drove hundreds of miles across the Stuart Highway, through a burning flat red desert with dusty riverbeds. I rarely saw another car. Finally, nearly ten thousand miles from where I lived, I would begin to find my way home.

The next morning, an hour before first light, I climbed the 1,100-foot Ayers Rock, called *Uluru* by the Aborigines. As I hauled myself past the last link of chain and took my final steps to the summit, a hot, dry wind caught the sweat of my face. Breathing hard from the last leg of the ascent, I slowly rose over the top. Below, in every direction, a stunning panorama of flat red desert spread to the horizon, as if reaching to the ends of the earth. Standing there alone on the highest peak of desolation, my mind suddenly drifted home—to my divorce, to my young children, to the challenge of running a company in the midst of my life's mess. And I realized that no matter how far we transport our bodies, our thoughts and worries are never far behind.

It had to be found, the source of one's own Self, one must possess
it! Everything else was seeking, was detour, was aberration.

I returned to the Castle of Doom in the suburbs of Chicago. A phone call soon brought a ray of light from the outside world: A friend introduced me to a gorgeous girl from Germany, who was doing an internship at a downtown Chicago bank. Smitten and lonely, I drove to the city each week to see her, visiting museums, strolling the lakefront, having dinner and drinks, dancing in stiflingly crowded clubs 'til the wee hours, and finishing with nightcaps. Of course, I told her my story.

My business friends, to whom I'd introduced her, all thought we were intimate. But the truth was, when I'd go to kiss her, she'd turn her head for a peck on the cheek. Having not dated in more than 13 years, much less a European, I didn't understand the protocol.

At the end of summer, she left for business school in London, with me still not clear if the relationship had potential. I stopped to see her after a business trip to Rust-Oleum's manufacturing plant in Holland. After two more days of cat-and-mouse strolling Picadilly Circus and hearing the London Philharmonic, I finally asked her straight out if she was attracted to me. Well, no, she said. And then proceeded to confess she'd been living with her boyfriend and having an affair with the guy across the hall. I suppose the Universe let out a good laugh at that point, but I hit a new low.

The divorce proceedings still languished, with my wife now making a motion for divorce not for "irreconcilable differences" but "mental abuse." That wouldn't fly either, though we might both be certifiably insane for continuing to live together in the Castle of Doom.

For one blessed week I had a respite from the divorce wars when Sally left to visit her parents. As I walked by the guestroom where Sally was staying, I noticed a small metal file box on the floor, about a foot long by eight inches wide and high. Curious, I took a closer look at the unlocked box, flipped the latch, and opened it. Out fell a love poem by the 17th century English writer John Donne, dedicated by Tim to Sally. The rest of the box was stuffed full of cards and letters. I carefully pulled out one letter, marking the spot so I could return it to its exact location. It too was from Tim, a love letter. They were all from Tim. Yikes! A treasure trove!

Now keep in mind, at this point, nearly a year into our divorce, I still didn't know how long their affair had been going on before I found out about it. I didn't know how it started. And I didn't think Sally and Tim had admitted the details to her attorney. Here were cards and letters dating back to at least seven months before the affair came to light.

My mind raced. What to do?

I took off for the office, where I could make copies of the cards and letters. Rust-Oleum headquarters remained mostly empty on that Saturday afternoon, except for a couple of die-hards doing their homework in the marketing department. We traded a wave and smile as I made my way to my corner office and closed the door. One by one, I carefully took a card or letter out of the box, turning the next one up-ended so I didn't lose my place. One by one, I read the contents.

Two hours later, I took my stack of copies and the metal file box and headed home.

Just then, a thought occurred to me, rising up from anger and resentment. I took a detour.

At the Hawthorne Shopping Mall, down the street from Rust-Oleum headquarters, I found a stand selling roses. I bought one. Something pulled me toward the adjacent Barnes & Noble bookstore. I walked in. There on an end-cap display in the front of the store: a poetry book by John Donne. Go figure. I bought it. Back home, I inscribed the cover page, "With love, Don" and tucked the rose inside. That's all I left in the box. The bomb had been planted. I'd launched a new front in the divorce war.

Not a word from Sally when she returned from her trip. But a day later, I received a letter from her attorney accusing me of opening a "locked box" in her room and demanding the return of its contents. No problem, my attorney responded: As long as the contents are entered into the court as official documents.

Soon afterwards, 15 months since the explosion of our marriage, the court officially established grounds for the divorce. One down, two to go—financial settlement and custody. Little did I know I still had nearly a year and a half of battles ahead of me.

And of course, what I'd just done only created more animosity, more distance, more hurt, and contributed to the long delay. The courts could care less about the details of their affair, and establishing grounds did little but fire the legal starting gun. Yes, I'd launched another front in the war out of spite, but gained only a Pyrrhic victory. Salmon don't consider consequences; they just fight their way upstream.

Curious, isn't it, that when relationships run aground, we can develop such intense feelings of hate towards people we once loved? Why is that? Where does the love go? Is it that people have changed and we no longer recognize them, or that we have changed and left them behind? Either way, it seems the intensity of emotion remains, with the only choice being whether we direct it in positive ways or negative.

Anger is always a secondary emotion, the result of an underlying feeling we haven't accepted or recognized, like fear, hurt, sadness, embarrassment, or shame. When we lose someone we love— whether through a breakup or death—indeed our love has lost its receptacle. Our reality suddenly changes. What we thought was true, the foundation on which we based our life, crumbles away. We go into free fall.

> I fight to hold on, I fight to let go, I fight to hold on,
> And it feels like my love has nowhere left to go.
> Fear holds on...love lets go.

—Stacey Fergusson, "Love Lets Go," Vanaka's *Gratitude* album

Fear makes us hold on to whatever we can, as a means of avoiding what we don't want to accept. Fear—or the range of other emotions that rush in to fill the void of love departing—emerges as intense anger, proportional to the love that was lost.

I ultimately realized that my intense anger was also fueled by my own failure to take responsibility for the dishonorable way in which my relationship with Sally first began. I fell in love with her my senior year, when my girlfriend of three years, Sue, left our college to attend graduate school in a distant city. Sally was one of Sue's best friends. While I had tried to end the relationship with Sue, she resisted. Fear held on for both us—fear of loss, fear of conflict. I was in two relationships for six months, and Sue was unaware of my affair with Sally. When it finally came time to choose, and tell the truth, I chose Sally. I didn't set out to hurt Sue. I just didn't know how to let go. And now I could more than imagine the pain it caused her since I was on the receiving end of the exact same behavior.

As winter approached, our divorce stalled. We still argued over custody. We still lived together in the Castle of Doom. I'd fired two divorce attorneys, one for dragging his feet and the other for not doing what I'd told him to do.

Yeah, I should have known better about a lot of things. But I can't *shoulda*. I only knew what I knew.

It would still be years before I learned *Siddhartha Principle One*: **ACCEPT. Meet yourself where you are, without judgment**.

Holding on to anger is like grasping a hot coal with the intent of throwing it at someone else; you are the one who gets burned.

—Buddha

Chapter 4: You Can't Do That

This bird, which used to sing in the morning hour, had become
mute, and once he noticed this, he stepped up to the cage and
looked inside; there was the little bird dead lying stiff on the
floor. He took it out, weighed it in his hand for a moment, and
then threw it away, out into the alley, and in the same instant he
became terribly frightened, and his heart ached, as if with this
dead bird, he had cast all value and all good away from him.

I moved through the beginning of winter, numb. As I look back,
it's hard to believe my circumstances had grown so dark, and I'd
been drawn down by the swirling eddies of loss, fear and grief.
As the scared Salmon, swimming like hell against the current of
my life, I'd become obsessed with the divorce proceedings and
collapsed into a state of self-righteousness, depression, and anxiety.
I needed a good friend to tell me, "You can't do that" and snap me
out of my funk.

I'd been a member of the Chicago chapter of the Young
Presidents Organization, joining a forum group six months after
my marriage blew up. The group was happy to have me. Fresh meat.
Juicy story. Comprised of a dozen other chapter members, my YPO
forum created a safe space to share life's challenges and successes.
The other members had also become presidents of large businesses
at an early age and, like me, had few close confidantes. We provided
extraordinary support and counsel to each other.

Eighteen months into the Great Divorce War, I attended a forum
meeting in Chicago. I hadn't shared the details of my divorce
proceedings, nor did I that day. But my frustration and negativity
emerged front and center as I updated the group on the latest and
not-so-greatest goings-on of my life. I got some feedback from

Mike Waters, one of my closest forum buddies: "You know," he said, "you're too nice a guy to let this divorce eat you up like this."

Mike's words hit me hard. I'd been swimming so hard in one direction, fueled by self-righteousness and fear, I couldn't see it another way. Now I stopped in mid-stroke. The Salmon flailed, tired. I knew deep down Mike was right. Finally, I had met myself where I was, and it didn't look pretty.

I decided it was time to stop dragging my feet and to get the divorce over with.

Earlier that month, I'd taken a lease on a downtown apartment, with a view of Lake Michigan, now frozen with the bitter cold of winter. I drove from store to store through the slushy streets of Chicago to find three cushy beige leather couches for the living room, the only furniture to fill this place. Those sofas sat there in a "U" looking silently out on the grey city, as if waiting for company.

It would be a long wait.

No one had the phone number. I wouldn't tell another soul about the place. Here hid my secret refuge, my every-so-often escape hatch from the Castle of Doom.

As winter wore on and the Salmon turned belly up, I came to grips with the reality of my divorce. The only reason I was staying in the house was the daily interaction with my children. Ever since they were little, I had given them a bath at night, read them bedtime stories, told them stories I made up, and then sang them songs like the Beatles' "Rocky Racoon" and "Yellow Submarine." We ended each night with James Taylor's "Close Your Eyes," with lyrics that refer to singing the song when I'm gone. Now I couldn't sing that line without a lump in my throat and tears coming to my eyes. For more than 18 months, I'd been living in fear of losing them in the divorce, and I fought letting go of that chapter of my life.

Fighting for full custody of the children would involve a long, grueling battle with little chance of success. Not in the children's best interest. The house? I could give it up. Too many ghosts. And with no end in sight for the divorce, I just couldn't keep living like this. Despite my attorneys crying, "You Can't Do That," I decided that as a birthday present to myself, on a Sunday in February, I would abandon ship.

But not without some cargo.

I didn't need much. My clothes, of course, but more importantly my music and my wine. Got to have priorities! No problem moving out with my collection of albums, CDs, and the speakers I'd had since I left college. But the wine bottles in the cellar? Now, that posed a challenge, particularly since I'd decided to move out in secret. I wasn't ready to tell my children, and honestly, I dreaded holding that conversation. I knew how upsetting it would be to them, and that it would make it harder for me to do what, deep in my heart, I knew had to be done.

To set the plan in motion, I made a phone call to John, my friend who owned a local wine store. On Sunday morning, while Sally attended church with the children, John arrived with a van. He went to work packing the cellar while I packed the rest of my items. Until in the middle of it all, John came with disturbing news from the front: "Don," he said, "I didn't bring enough boxes. I can come back tomorrow for the rest of it."

"No! There is no tomorrow," I said with a panicked seriousness. "I've got to get it all out NOW! We've got to get this done today— and we only have a couple more hours!"

I knew Sally planned to take the children to a church picnic right after the services, so I figured I had until mid-afternoon. John thought for a minute. "OK, I've got more boxes at my store. I can be there and back in maybe 40 minutes."

"Go!" I said, my mind racing, doing the math on the ticking clock. John tore down the driveway. And not a minute later…here came Sally!

Terror struck. *What's she doing back here?* Yikes! Hide!

I fled to my bedroom, closed and locked the door. I phoned John. "Don't come back until you hear from me," I instructed, with no idea of when or if. I waited silently. Then came a knock at my door. "Dad, are you in there? Dad?" My two children were looking for me. I held my breath. Tall cardboard clothes boxes crowded my room. Agonizing seconds hung in the air.

Sally called to them from the back hallway. "Come on, guys, picnic time. Let's go."

I heard my children scamper down the stairs. "Dad didn't answer," my ten-year-old daughter said.

My heart ached. *Hiding from my children?* I had planned to talk with them later that night, after I'd put the move behind me. Now I felt the full weight of my decision. *How can I abandon them?* Dread and panic rose to my throat, tears welled in my eyes. The feeling of guilt became almost overwhelming.

OK, snap out of it, I told myself. *I can't stay here anymore.* They say: Put your oxygen mask on first, then you can help your children. I needed to breathe. The children would be alright.

I called John. The coast was clear. Resume Operation Escape!

At 3 p.m, John was finished. "I'll get your wine into storage tomorrow. Let me know when you want them back."

"It'll be a long time, John," I replied. "I don't have a place for them. And I don't know when I will."

That evening, I sat with my children and cried. Daddy was moving to another house, I explained. Mommy and I couldn't keep living here together. I would still see them every week. I loved them and wouldn't be far away.

Then I drove down the snow-covered driveway, glancing back through the rearview mirror at the lights of the Castle of Doom glowing through the darkness of winter. I took a deep breath. I sobbed. For me, for my children, for the dreams in ashes. I couldn't imagine life without seeing my kids every day. A month later, my son brought this home from school in his 7-year-old handwriting and spelling, entitled "My Dad:"

My dad maks the best pankaks. My dad does not live in my house. My dad works at Rust-Oleum. My dad liks to go fishing. My dad is renting a house. My dad is very nice. I love you dad.

It really brought home the loss. But I knew I had to meet myself where I was. Divorce has consequences, and the toughest is the impact on the children. The kids would survive the separation and so would I. I resolved to move on and build a new life with my children and a new life for myself. I worked out a visitation schedule with Sally: having my children with me every other weekend and each Wednesday evening.

I'd lost my wife, my best friend, and other friends who'd sided with my wife and Tim. I'd lost my home, missed the close relationship I'd had with Sally's family, and was separated from my children. I was lonely and depressed. I knew I needed to rebuild my life, and I longed to have some companionship, but I didn't have a clue how to approach a new intimate relationship after having been out of the dating world for 15 years.

I met my first girlfriend, Linda, at a business conference. Two weeks later, she flew into Chicago for a visit, then we made plans to rendezvous for a weekend in Las Vegas. But honestly, I had no idea how to date. It's laughable: In preparation for the Vegas trip, I bought silk pajamas and a robe. Eat your heart out, Hugh Hefner. By the end of the weekend I'd fallen hopelessly in love, certain that this was the one.

An old friend told me differently. "I'm happy for you. Have fun. But I'd be willing to bet you're going to have at least fifteen relationships until you find the one to marry."

I thought he was crazy, but instead he was oddly prophetic.

He, who was still a boy in regards to love, and tended to throw
himself blindly and voraciously into pleasure as into the abyss,
was taught by her from the ground up the lesson that you
can not take pleasure without giving pleasure. Every gesture,
every caress, every touch, every look, every smallest spot of the
body has its secret, which to reveal brings happiness to the one
who understands. He became her pupil, her lover, her friend.
Here lay the value and meaning of his current life.

I met my furthest long-distance relationship, Jessica, on my first trip to Australia. In Phoenix, I reunited with Sara, a girlfriend from high school, who remained a girlfriend from high school. In Aspen, I met Anna, the sister of a famous Olympian, for a short but sizzling sprint. A friend set me up with two women in LA. In Chicago, I dated a public relations director for a local theater, a mortgage broker, a curator for the art museum, the manager of an upscale home décor shop, a senior at the University of Illinois, a Russian artist, and a financial consultant. I thought each might be "The One."

My longest stint, lasting nearly a year, involved a sweet young woman named Pam. I met her at a dude ranch in Colorado where I took my children on vacation. At age 22, she was 17 years my junior. My God, I think the Beatles broke up before she was born. Cute, blonde, gorgeous green eyes, a big white smile, Pam told me on the first date at my Chicago Place condo that she had something to show me: on her left hip just above her butt cheek, a 4-inch high tattoo of a wolf—with green eyes. If this was my mid-life crisis, bring it on. Before long, we had both fallen headlong in love. She became my every-weekend companion, one of the few girlfriends I introduced to my children.

At one point, Pam and my two children piled into the back of a taxi in Chicago, I got in front with the driver, and he looked back and asked, "Your children?" A voice in my head said the gap might be too wide to bridge. I soon ended the relationship, but was deeply grateful for learning from her what it felt like to be unconditionally loved by a romantic partner.

After several years in the dating game, I finally came to this conclusion: Relationships are for learning. I learned that I'm happier by myself than I am in a relationship that isn't right. I learned the importance of clarifying my values and finding a woman who shares them. I learned that a wonderful and long-lasting sexual relationship only evolves from an authentic and emotionally intimate one.

If I had learned some of these lessons a bit earlier in life—though I know you can't do that—I might have been able to create and sustain a healthier marriage, or when confronted with an inevitable divorce, end it more quickly and less painfully. And end it did, not with a bang, but a whimper.

Month after month, the judge had postponed our trial date, an effective tactic employed to avoid hearing cases. Perhaps she'd hoped that we'd eventually get frustrated—or tired enough of paying legal fees—and settle out of court. On the day of our trial, we had dragged box after box of documents into the courtroom. Then the judge told us she didn't have time to hear the case that day—we'd have to postpone again. But with all the attorneys there for the big trial, we'd have none of it. We declared we were going to work out the settlement NOW. By the end of the day, we had an agreement.

After all the drama, my Salmon approach hadn't generated anything except lots of aggravation, anger, and big legal bills. Granted, I'd gained self-confidence, become tougher, and learned to delegate more and work less. But as far as the divorce was concerned, I'd spent two and half years of my life with little more to show than long-lasting resentment and no restitution. As best I could tell at that time, my waking nightmare of two-and-a-half years earlier had come true: Sally and Tim moved into what was my former house with our children and a lot of my former money.

Even with a large settlement, the final negotiation came down to whether Sally would get the dining room chandelier that my mother had given us as a gift (she did). Looking back, had I taken the Siddhartha approach, observed and accepted the realities of my situation, and asserted myself to gain a positive settlement without all the self-righteous anger, I would have saved time and money, encouraged a civil relationship with my ex-wife, and kept my children out of the crossfire. Maybe I'd even have gotten that chandelier!

Chapter 5: You Can't Do That, Either

*Then Siddhartha knew that the game was over, and
that he could no longer play it. A shiver ran through his body;
inside, he felt, something had died.*

An interesting thing happens when we go through a crisis in one area of our life: We start looking at what else isn't working.

Just after dawn at 6:30 one October morning, nearly a year after my divorce, I walked into my office, looked at the pile of papers on my desk, and said out loud to myself: "I don't want to do this anymore." The words rose from deep in my heart and shook me.

But still, I questioned my sanity. *You're president of a great company, one voice in my head said. Most people would kill to have your job. And you're the third generation. What would the Captain think? What would your father think? What about the future of your children? How could you sell the legacy of your family? You can't do that!*

Another voice in my head replied, *But I'm not happy. Is this all there is for the rest of my life?*

I called Morrie Shechtman, my counselor. "Morrie, I think I'm losing my mind. I might have made a decision this morning to sell the company. I need to talk with you right away. Can you come by this afternoon for a while?"

"I can be there at one o'clock for the rest of the afternoon, if that works for you," he said. "And, by the way, I don't think you're crazy. This might be the sanest thing you've done in a long time."

As a mid-sized company, Rust-Oleum Corporation faced sizeable risks. Our main competitors loomed much larger, and the industry was consolidating. Our family shareholders didn't have much appetite for making big acquisitions or taking on debt. Being a chemical company, we faced myriad government regulations that raised our costs and threatened our future viability. We'd incurred big losses on the failures of two major new-product ventures that attempted to diversify the company.

Despite these major challenges with new products, we had enjoyed five years of consecutive record sales and operating profits in our core business. I just wasn't confident we could keep it going.

I held a minority position, couldn't afford to buy out the rest of the family, and feared committing the next 30 years of my life to the company while always wondering when the others might one day want to sell at an inopportune time—or not sell when I wanted out. I considered hanging in there to preserve the opportunity for my children, but they were only 12 and 9, and it would be a long time before I knew if they turned out to have both interest and capability in someday running the company. And did I really want to saddle them with an even smaller minority ownership?

I went through all of this with Morrie that October afternoon.

"First of all, there are some major challenges with my executive team," I shared with Morrie. "I've got some officers who have become comfortable in place and aren't doing a great job of growing the business. I'm also concerned about my minority position if I try to make major leadership changes."

"So," Morrie replied, "you could launch into battle with your Executives, the Board, and other family members to gain greater leverage. Then you could change out and revitalize your executive team, which is no small task. And what allies do you have to accomplish all that?"

I looked at him blankly and shook my head.

"Assuming I got through all of that in the next couple of years," I responded, "I still face a daunting competitive and regulatory environment, risky diversification strategies, and no guarantee of success. The company's seen five years of record profits and there's a strong acquisition market. I could sell the company for maximum value right now."

"Given all that, do you still think it's crazy to sell the business?" Morrie asked.

"No," I admitted. "It makes a lot of sense. And I'm tired, Morrie. I don't have the energy to fight all those battles with few allies."

On Christmas Eve, while many were stuffing stockings and wrapping presents, I worked alone at the office until 3 a.m. preparing additional documents that would dissolve the Board, appoint me as Chairman, and create a new Board consisting of five voting trustees, each of whom had been entrusted with a 20 percent vote to approve the eventual sale: myself, my sister, my two cousins, and a representative of the bank which held 40 percent of the shares in trust from my father's and uncle's estates. By the January Board meeting, I'd fired the shot, announced the sale, completed the sales brochure on the company, and launched a full-scale auction. By April, we had a signed agreement with RPM, Inc. to purchase Rust-Oleum Corporation for the target value I'd promised the shareholders.

At that point, it really settled in on me that soon, at the ripe old age of 41, I would no longer have a job or a family company. No business card. No official identity. No longer "Mr. Rust-Oleum." I'd been swimming so hard, I hadn't taken the time to reflect on what this really meant. I didn't have the energy to figure out *what next*. I could only swim hard away from what was.

I stared out the window of my condo, all alone one weekend night, sipping a single-malt Scotch, as spring drizzle misted the lights along Michigan Avenue. *My God, what have I done?*, I wondered darkly. More importantly, *What will I do now?* My life stretched before me as a blank slate, frightening in its lack of boundaries. And at the same time, I sensed profound relief waiting in the wings. What would it be like not to worry about the future of aerosol paint, or about losing a major account? I realize now, the Siddhartha deep within me had faith that the answers would come.

The deal closed in June. After a nine-month marathon, part war and part chess game, through repeated cries of "You Can't Do That," I had done it. For better or worse, I had abandoned ship and headed off in my life raft for destinations unknown. Liberated from the weight, I came unmoored in my life.

Chapter 6: Love Me Do

Once he said to her: "You are like me; you are different from
most people. You are Kamala, nothing else, and within you
there is a silence and a shelter to which you can turn at every
hour and be at home with yourself, just as I can. Few people
have this, and yet it is something everyone could have."

Six months before closing the sale of the company, I had spent a
snowy Christmas alone. My ex-wife had the children, and I had five
girlfriends—two in Chicago, one in Aspen, one in LA and one in
Perth, Australia. In the process of dating for nearly three years, I'd
clarified what I wanted in a woman, but hadn't yet found Ms. Right.
In fact, I started a list on that first trip to Australia two years earlier,
when I'd penned my wishes on *The Regent Sydney* stationery:

Cares for me deeply.
Loyal, high integrity, honest.
Spirit of adventure—enjoys learning & trying new things.
Independent, not overly dependent on me.
Shares an interest in art, music.
Love of the outdoors and outdoor activities, involving the water, sun, and
mountains.
Intelligent, thoughtful.
Spiritual.
Uninhibited sexuality.
Vivacious, outgoing, extroverted.

But most importantly, I'd come to define a great relationship as two
people "independently happy together." That's code for: Both people
take responsibility for their own happiness rather than depending
on the other person to create it for them.

Through 14 relationships, I'd been swimming like a Salmon heading upriver on his last run. Though I'd met some lovely women, none quite fit the bill. I finally gave up on ever finding "the one," and decided I might as well just have fun. That seemed like progress. At least the Salmon had a smile on his face.

Funny how life works: Just as I gave up ever finding Ms. Right, she appeared.

Unbeknownst to me, a friend had an inkling that I'd like Stacey Johnson. She'd worked for him in Los Angeles for nearly ten years.

Every few months since my divorce, he would ask Stacey, "What about my buddy Don?" She would wisely decline. *I think he needs to have a few relationships first*, she'd think to herself. In the meantime, she went to work as a personal assistant for producer Aaron Spelling, to whom she referred affectionately as "Mister," eventually becoming household manager, based in their 55,000-square-foot mansion near Beverly Hills. For two years, she answered his phone, read scripts, managed the household staff, and even went on vacation with the family to Las Vegas, chaperoning teenaged Tori. Then, Stacey got the call from my friend.

"Hey…what about my buddy Don?"

Stacey thought about it. She'd just ended a relationship.

"Okay, I figure he's been divorced a couple years and had a few relationships by now. I know he's a nice guy. I'm ready for that. You can give him my number."

Over the next two months, I talked with her frequently by phone, intrigued. She seemed independent, never pausing for a long conversation before heading off to photograph a band, spend time with her girlfriends, or find another reason to leave me wanting more. Stacey laughed easily and shared my love of travel and adventure. She also shared my beliefs about spirituality. We agreed relationships worked best with a combination of independence and togetherness. She shared her upset about her former boyfriend, yet saw the failed relationship as a lesson to respect herself more. I loved the sound of her voice, and still hadn't seen a picture.

In the meantime, for my forty-first birthday that February, the snowfall whitened the night outside as I dined by warm candlelight at a small French restaurant in the Chicago suburbs with the Russian artist who claimed lineage to the last Czar.

The next day found me on a date with the sister of a famous Olympian. The weekend brought a flight to LA for a blind date with the mysterious Stacey, to be followed the next night by a second date with a swim teacher. I checked into my hotel and waited for Stacey's arrival.

The knock came. I strode across the foyer, opened the door, and met her beautiful blue eyes and her warm smile framed by shoulder-length blond hair. Without thinking, we hugged and kissed hello. It seemed natural, not forward. Our conversation flowed easily, and over a candlelit dinner in Beverly Hills, I paid little attention to the food or wine. We stayed up all night in my suite, talking and laughing. As the first light of dawn cast a glow on the drapes, I looked in her eyes and blurted, "You're just like me. I love you. Will you marry me?" She laughed. So did I. But from the depths of my soul, Siddhartha knew I wasn't kidding.

I cancelled my date for the following night to spend more time with Stacey. When I returned to Chicago, I broke up with all my girlfriends.

ᔐ

Slowly walking, Siddhartha pondered...He observed that something had left him behind, like the snake shedding its old skin, that something was not present in him anymore, something that had accompanied and belonged to him throughout his youth...

After the nine-month chess game of selling the company, and the four-year marathon to get to happy since the demise of my marriage, finding Stacey couldn't have felt closer to heaven. With the merger papers signed and my desk cleaned out, I had a Get Out of Jail Free card from my personal Monopoly game. Pass Go, collect my dollars, and go directly to…wherever I wanted.

But what do I put on the immigration form under "Occupation"?

For 41 years, my identity had been intertwined with Rust-Oleum. Now I didn't have a business card. How do I answer the question, "So, what do you *do*?" Granted that's a first world problem.

However, it also introduces a secondary problem. Those who become overly focused on what they do, even if they have the financial means and flexibility to make major career and life changes, often stay stuck in a life that no longer makes them happy. I've known many a mogul who "arrived" at the top of their game—more money than God, big home, vacation houses, airplanes, boats—and a life that has long since spun out of balance. Health? Forget it. Constant stress, no exercise, a bad diet and a good bit of drinking concoct a recipe for high cholesterol, stomach ailments and heart problems. Marriage? The spouse seems more roommate than lover. Work life? Bored or burned out. At mid-life, these highly capable performers really don't need to work anymore, but they keep on swimming like a Salmon.

Why? Well, some just thrive on the adrenaline rush, want to make a difference in the world, love the feeling of accomplishment or admiration that comes with business success, or feel responsible to others. But many keep swimming because they don't know what they'd *do* or who they'd *be* if they weren't in that river.

No doubt, I jumped out of the river partly because I could, financially. That made my choice easier. But the voice of Siddhartha whispered to me the kinds of questions that might occur to any working person at a major turning point in life:

Why am I doing this? Am I motivated by obligation or inspiration, fear or love? In the bigger picture of life, what's my end game? What's truly important to me? What brings me deep happiness? And is this river taking me there? I had to face the fear of the unknown, and I sensed there was more of life to discover.

When I returned home, the Salmon in me still felt the need to swim, subtly battling guilty discomfort whenever someone asked, "So what do you *do?*" I thought I'd experiment with "being of service" as an answer to that question, so I volunteered as president of a charitable organization. After all, I knew how to manage and I could leverage my business network. Indeed, after the first year, I got kudos raising a record $300,000 for a women's hospital in Chicago.

It took me the better part of that year to realize I'd taken the job because it allowed me to claim (to myself and others) that I was a valuable person. Having successfully completed the first year's fund-raising gala, I bailed out on a second year, realizing I needed to face the void of my life without a major commitment on my plate.

I also wanted to spend more time at a home I'd bought in southern California during the middle of the Rust-Oleum sale. If and when the company sold, I realized I didn't have to live full-time in the Chicago suburbs. I'd come to dread the interminable, cold, dreary winters, and the hot, humid, mosquito-infested summers. I'd agreed to the terms of our custody arrangement back when I had a full-time job—"visitation" every other weekend plus dinner with the children Wednesday evenings—and my ex-wife wouldn't budge to give me more time. Did I really want to have a house close to my children, in a place I didn't love, when I would still only see them 15% of my time? Or was there another way to maintain my close relationship with them, and be happy the other 85%, too?

I'd come to know Southern California when I first started dating Stacey. On the beaches in February, bikinied girls and tan guys played volleyball on the beach, and surfers plied the waves. Back home, Lake Michigan was frozen over. *If I'm going to have a new life,* I thought, *this sure looks like a good start.* I figured I could rearrange my visitation schedule to come into Illinois for a weekend with my children, stay at the Chicago condo during the week, driving to the suburbs to see my children for Wednesday dinner, and get my children for the following weekend as well. Then I'd go back to California or travel elsewhere, keeping in touch by phone.

Having a home halfway across the country from my children pushed the edge of my comfort zone as a father and no doubt challenged them to deal with the reality of divorce. Oftentimes, getting to "acceptance" at the end of a grieving process is a matter of "making the choice that sucks the least." Perhaps there's also a fine line between self-centered and self-honoring, but I needed to create my new life. I gave myself permission to breathe, and we all came to appreciate *quality* time more than quantity. When we were together, we were fully together, without distractions. We played board games, visited museums, enjoyed Gino's East pizza, took carriage rides, and laughed a lot. It was always sad when it came time to drive them home on Sunday night. But in many ways, we gained more closeness *because* of our distance. And Southern California gave my children valuable experiences like boogie-boarding, kayaking with dolphins, and coming to know a world beyond the Illinois suburbs.

He looked around, as though seeing the world for the first time.
The world was beautiful, the world was colorful, the world
was strange and mysterious. Here was blue, here was yellow, here
was green, sky flowed and river, forest gaped and mountains,
all beautiful, full of mystery and magical, and in the midst of all
he, Siddhartha, awakening on the path to himself.

Chapter 7: Baby Love

It was the Self whose meaning and essence I wanted to learn.

From the time I met Stacey, I knew she was "The One." Still, two things I *couldn't* imagine doing included:

1. Getting married again.

2. Having another child.

After dating Stacey for six months, in the flood of romantic love, I bought a diamond ring that I thought might buy me a bit of time before having to actually take the vows. I planned to pop the question in the middle of August, just weeks after selling the company. As I pondered my plans for "tying the knot," I began to feel an imaginary noose tighten around my neck. *Am I sure she's the one? What if this doesn't work out? I sure don't want to go through another divorce.*

I admit I was terrified of making a major mistake. It had been less than two years since I finished painful divorce proceedings. I panicked, and as Stacey's consolation prize, I bought her a necklace with matching earrings. For her birthday the following week, Stacey got the gift—and soon after, my request for a co-habitation agreement.

After nearly two years, I eventually gained more confidence to take the plunge. Well, sort of...

At the end of a candlelight dinner, I mustered my courage. Out came a small box with that diamond ring, and a letter for Stacey— with the lyrics to a Todd Rundgren song, *Mated*, which alluded to being together for life without being married.

I asked her to marry me...someday. Yeah, that's right. I still could only go as far as "engagement" without committing to *when* or *ever*. My ring signified commitment, and I hoped it would buy me some time. Though I loved Stacey and truly wanted to demonstrate my commitment to her, I was still shell-shocked from divorce and skeptical of the institution of marriage.

In fact, it would be three more years before we'd marry. My wake-up call came when Stacey's dad died suddenly of a heart attack, and through tears Stacey cried, "Now he'll never get a chance to walk me down the aisle." It finally became starkly clear to me that my fear was holding both of us back from living the lives we wanted.

⌒

> Then suddenly, this also had become clear to him:
> He, who indeed was like one awakened or newly born,
> must start his life anew and completely from the beginning.

We married at our home in Southern California, veering away from the traditional path. Often at weddings, people come from near and far, but the bride and groom are so busy with arrangements—and it all goes by so quickly—it seems all there's time to do is have a hug and a handshake, a short chat, and dance to "Celebration." So, instead of a one-day event, we planned a long weekend, beginning with an evening boat cruise where we could greet our guests, catch up on our lives, and connect with our friends and family. We'd have the wedding on Saturday afternoon, a party that night; and on Sunday, guests could join us around the pool at home. We held our wedding outdoors, and live music filled the day. In order to fully enjoy our time with our guests, and to simplify logistics, we postponed our honeymoon in Italy until two months later.

After returning from Tuscany, we flew to Montana for a couples retreat hosted by Morrie Shechtman and his therapist wife, Arleah, at their mountain home. Stacey and I loved each other and our relationship, and we wanted to keep it that way. Attending an intense workshop with four other couples for three days demonstrated our mutual commitment.

At the retreat, Morrie and Arleah asked each of us to share a disappointment. At my urging, Stacey confided one of hers: the likely prospect of not having a child of her own. For the past five years, any time Stacey would gingerly raise the possibility of the two of us having a baby, I'd shut down the conversation. "I already have two children," I'd say testily. "And besides, we both value travel, freedom and flexibility. That goes out the window when you have a kid."

The retreat resulted in Stacey and me realizing we both still had individual issues to address. We each signed up for separate, on-going sessions with Arleah, which continued for a year and a half.

Months after the retreat, I happened to see Morrie, who asked, "So, have you and Stacey had any more conversations about having a child together?"

"No," I confided. "We haven't really talked much about it."

"Why not?" Morrie asked.

"Well, I think Stacey is pretty much resigned to not having children, since it would really affect our relationship."

"Hmm, maybe you should have a conversation with her about that." Morrie replied. "It seems to me you're avoiding it."

I didn't have to raise the issue with Stacey. Coincidentally, soon after my conversation with Morrie, she asked me again if we could talk about having a child. This time, instead of accepting my standard response, *I already have two children, and besides...*, she pushed back.

"Listen, Don," she said firmly and sincerely, "I love you, and I don't want to run the risk that we never really talk this through, and I end up resenting you for it."

Bang. I realized my old pattern of avoiding conflict by angrily shutting down unpleasant conversations or killing feelings with logic. Wake up time. I opened the door to working this through.

We began by writing out a list of "pros" and "cons," as if logic would provide the answer. (OK, so this was my idea.) Still far apart, we agreed to keep revisiting the conversation every few weeks.

Guess what? In these continuing conversations, we realized that the surface issue wasn't the issue. Simply weighing the pros and cons of how a child might change our lifestyle didn't address the underlying fears and irrational beliefs that kept us stuck in old patterns of thinking and feeling. In order to discover and shift these patterns, we needed to dig a lot deeper.

We'd have to face regret no matter what we decided. There was no doubt Stacey loved my children, and our quality times together had forged deep bonds with them. She had become their "Bonus Mom" and a loving and caring friend. But just as Stacey wouldn't replace their real mom, being a part-time mom to my children couldn't replace the experience of raising one of her own. She'd always pictured herself as a mother, and it hurt to give up that dream. I knew with a child, we'd give up the freedom to travel on a moment's whim, and it might change the free-spirited nature of our intimate relationship. Deep down, I feared the loss of romance in our marriage with the emergence of diapers, PTA and play dates. We both agreed that neither of us should sacrifice our self to the other, and we needed to embrace whatever decision we made. But how would we come to a compromise when she wanted a child and I didn't, when if she won, I lost or vice-versa?

Though at this time I had not yet formalized the 5 Siddhartha Principles, I had begun to practice several new approaches to live with greater awareness and create more of what I wanted. In this instance, the first step involved living with the conflict—*Siddhartha Principle One:* **ACCEPT. Meet yourself where you are, without judgment.** A Salmon feels compelled to push ahead to a quick solution. Siddhartha remains patient, knowing the true value lies in the *process* itself and what we learn from it, that is *Siddhartha Principle Two:* **LEARN. Find the lesson in your present challenge.** We both knew that how we *related* to each other while we were going through the conflict was more important than how it got resolved.

As I dug deeper, I discovered two great fears:

1. A child would pull Stacey away from me, as her focus shifted from lover to mother, and

2. If our marriage didn't work out, a divorce would be even more costly and painful.

Yes, the biggest obstacles to me having a child with Stacey were artifacts from my previous marriage and "negative future fantasies" about hypothetical losses. Just getting married again had seemed scary. Having a child would represent an even deeper commitment—and risk.

I had to admit that the relationship with Stacey was nothing like what I'd created in my first marriage. I'd replicated in my first marriage the lack of genuine emotional expression I'd experienced in my family as a child. (Interesting how we tend to recreate emotional dynamics because they're familiar, not necessarily good for us.) Up until this point, I avoided conflict instead of using it for greater understanding, and I lacked a familial model for open and expressive affection. As I looked back on my first marriage, I incorrectly associated having children with a distancing between my wife and me, as life as a family became more complex than life as a couple. In reality, back then I didn't know how to create emotional intimacy in the first place. My real job now was to avoid projecting this old pattern onto Stacey or a new child.

The lights came on. Stacey wasn't Sally, I could make different choices in this relationship, having children did not contribute to the breakdown of my previous marriage, and…I really enjoyed fatherhood. In fact, my life would lack so much richness if my children weren't part of it. I only wished they could have been more a part of it, instead of having the separation caused by the divorce.

Stacey, too, went about her inner work, trying to understand why having a child was important to her, and if having a child really was a requirement for a fulfilling life. She explored her own childhood and family dynamics—the joys and triumphs and the unmet expectations and losses. She examined her fears and motives of having a child (or not), asking herself questions: "Is this my true voice…or just fear talking? Is this society or someone else projecting what is best for me? Will a child bring me unconditional love?"

As we both came to our individual realizations, our "kid issue" became less emotionally charged. Still, the process took more than a year. Stacey had accepted that we might not have a child, though she still wanted one. I continued to wrestle with my fear that a child would pull us apart. That Thanksgiving, we were joined by our good friends Adde and Mike Waters. Mike was the YPO forum buddy who years ago had given me insight about letting go of anger in my divorce. They asked us if we'd made any decisions about having a child. Stacey explained the inner process she'd been going through, and with tears in her eyes, confided she didn't think we'd have a child. At that moment, I saw how much loss Stacey would feel with that decision. Suddenly, my love for Stacey grew bigger than my fear. I would act on faith. That night, I told her I'd made a decision: Let's go for it! Within two weeks, she was pregnant. Nine months later, we looked into the blue eyes of a wise old soul, a baby boy. Neither of us can imagine life without him.

The powerful lesson from this experience is that by taking the Siddhartha approach to conflict, we grow closer. Surprising gifts come when we can recognize and accept our emotions honestly, without judgment, delve below the surface issues to discover what's really driving the upset, and have the patience (and faith) to work through the process from a place of empathy and love.

Despite our intensive work, there was still much more for Stacey and me to learn. When our son first came home from the hospital, my worst fears began to surface. Stacey focused fully on him, of course, and this stirred my old "familiar" feelings of emotional abandonment. I started withdrawing (another old pattern). OK, I thought, *Stacey needs to focus on him. I guess I need to focus more on work. Life's gonna be different. Might as well get used to it.* I jumped deeper into marketing my new Couples' Retreat. The Salmon in me started swimming for the next goal line to avoid recognizing my hurt.

Fortunately, Stacey noticed my brooding. "Don, I think we need to have a date," she said. "My mom's going to spend a week with us to help with the baby, so while she's here, let's take a couple hours by ourselves and reconnect."

The next evening, while Stacey's mother tended the infant, Stacey and I retreated to our bedroom. "So, how are you feeling about having a baby?" I asked Stacey. She shared her excitement and her fears. A wonderful new chapter of our lives had begun, and at the same time, the responsibility seemed overwhelming. Stacey asked me the same question. I dug deep for honesty.

"Well, Stacey, I love our son. And I'm really scared that I might lose you and that our relationship might slip away." Tears came. "I know it sounds selfish. I know you need to focus on him right now," I continued. "But I can't help feeling afraid."

We agreed that our intimate relationship needed nurturing, just like the baby. It was time to employ *Siddhartha Principle Three:* **CLARIFY. Create an Ideal Scene of your desired experience.** Stacey and I agreed that our vision of the future included a vibrant romantic relationship and continued personal growth, while recognizing and embracing our new circumstances. We knew that only if we stayed close as a couple would we provide a strong foundation for parenting and family.

With our son only days old, we made the decision to set up a regular sitter every week, so Stacey and I would always have "date time" to reconnect emotionally and physically. We enter those dates on the calendar months in advance, and they aren't moveable without mutual agreement, so everything else has to fit in around them. It's our way of living what we say is important: the pre-eminence of our adult intimate relationship.

We don't use date time to go to movies or out to dinner. Those become "bonuses." In every home we've had, we've set aside a romantic "date space," very private from the rest of the house, sometimes as part of our sleeping room, decorated with cushy sofas, pillows, and lots of candles. We set aside a minimum of two hours, usually more, to talk about what's going on in our lives, discuss anything that's bothering us, and share our feelings. And we each know, our date will have a "happy ending." No guess work.

Here's the other axiom we've learned to follow: Sex *before* meals! (I petitioned for "sex before every meal," but I suppose that wasn't practical.) Our date time starts at three or four in the afternoon. After all, who's feeling energized and romantic at ten o'clock on a Friday night after a big meal and a bottle of wine? There's a big payoff in leaving work a little early and rearranging our days to prioritize our relationship.

Now, I've got to acknowledge right away that many couples don't have the luxury of extra space, some can't leave work early, and others have challenges with childcare. But most of the time, these are surface issues. If you value your relationship and agree to its priority, it forces an examination of the obstacles that stand in the way. Is your social schedule booked solid every night and through the weekends? How many hours do you spend at the office, and what really drives you to do that? Are you like the average American, watching over 30 hours of TV every week, and could you better utilize that time? In order to make self-honoring choices, to whom or to what might you have to say "no?" Do you use busyness to protect you from the fear of emotional intimacy?

I learned the hard way how much more time and energy it takes to go through divorce than to tackle these issues while I'm still in the marriage. Challenging each other to fully "show up" in a relationship —and carving out the time to invest in it—pays big dividends.

Once we establish what's truly important in our lives, like our intimate relationship, we must decide to live accordingly, *Siddhartha Principle Four:* **ACT. Take small steps to create your desired experience.** We get creative and strategize. How can we carve out date time and create a special romantic atmosphere in our home?

Move the work desk and clutter out of the corner of the bedroom. Go shopping together, to choose some romantic accents for the room. Pick a day during the week for a regularly scheduled date, and shift your schedule to have it at a time you're both awake and invigorated. Maybe that means a weekend morning. Or perhaps you set up a regular play date for the children on a weekend afternoon, so you can have a play date of your own. If you can't find a regular sitter, how about a family member, or trading time with friends who have children? Consider the possibility of leaving work early one afternoon each week or each month, coming home while the children are still at school.

And now, put these dates on your calendar for weeks ahead of time, so everything else has to be scheduled around them. When date time comes around, here are a few helpful guidelines:

1. **Set a time to meet, dressed and ready for play, and stick to it.** Don't make your lover wait. You don't want to start off agitated.

2. **Remember our rule: sex before meals!** Plan dinner ahead of time, so you don't end up hungry and scrambling for food at the conclusion of your romance. Consider having a pre-made meal in the fridge, or order in, so you don't have the time constraint of a restaurant reservation.

3. *Shower, shave and shine.* Do whatever it takes to smell fresh and be kissable by the time your date starts.

4. **Dress to impress.** Even if you stay home, dress like you're on a hot date. No couch potato sweats allowed!

5. **Create the atmosphere.** Set aside a certain area for your date and lovemaking. Clear clutter. Light candles. Throw some satin sheets over the furniture or bed. Choose a mutually agreed playlist.

During your date:

1. **No emails or phone calls,** unless you both agree they require immediate attention.

2. **Appetizers.** Prepare a tray of snacks, and include your choice of beverage.

3. **Reconnect.** Take time to share and listen to each other. Ask open-ended questions. Don't try to solve the other person's problems.

4. **Be playful.** Set an intention to laugh, have fun, and remember why you love this person!

Use your date time to make an emotional connection. Share what you're feeling at the moment about your individual challenges. Explore what you're learning about yourselves. Share your dreams and wildest fantasies for the future. Practice your listening skills by asking open-ended questions, empathetically hearing each other rather than trying to "fix" each other or solve problems.

When Stacey and I first started our practice of weekly dates, we would first get together a couple days in advance to share one thought on each of two questions: What have you observed me doing in the past week that you most admire or appreciate? What have you observed me doing that most concerns or bothers you? The first part of the conversation gave us a chance to do some mutual appreciation. When we catch each other doing something good, it tends to inspire more of the same. The second part gave us practice at "clearing the air," so neither of us withheld a grievance or concern from the other, which could end up festering if not addressed.

My suggestion for couples first practicing this method: Separate this conversation from date time. Establish a different time to share appreciation and concerns, perhaps a couple days prior to your date time. Set aside time and space so you won't be interrupted. Get yourself in a mental and emotional state of being open to feedback, without reacting defensively. Remember that feedback is simply information. It is a window into how your partner is perceiving you.

Use feedback to apply the first two *Siddhartha Principles*—

Siddhartha Principle One: **ACCEPT. Meet yourself where you are, without judgment.**

Siddhartha Principle Two: **LEARN. Find the lesson in your present challenge.**

One of the biggest killers of a relationship over time is apathy—not caring enough to engage in productive conflict, or not knowing how. Research shows that most relationships don't end because of having conflict. They end because distance creeps in, couples withdraw, and they lose their friendship. Giving and receiving feedback underscores how much we care about our relationships, and nurtures a deeper connection.

The simple "two question" method of providing feedback—what you admire or appreciate and what concerns or bothers you—helps insure that you and your partner consciously acknowledge each other and don't withhold grievances for long. But many conflict "conversations" aren't premeditated—they arise spontaneously, as we get triggered by something in the moment. So, in addition to building in some structured mechanisms for giving feedback, we need to become conscious of the way we respond to events in real time—and notice the patterns of responses that characterize our relationship—so that these "symptoms" don't become a disease that ultimately destroys the relationship.

Within five minutes of listening to a couple dealing with conflict, researcher John Gottman can predict with over 90 percent accuracy whether their marriage is doomed! He looks for the *pattern* I call The Danger Zone, characterized by the couple displaying:

Criticism—harsh attacks directed at the person rather than at their behavior.

Contempt—expressing disdain, disrespect, derision, scorn, or sarcasm.

Defensiveness—blaming the other, and acting the victim.

Withdrawal—shutting down, refusing to engage, or literally walking away from the conversation.

As I reflect on my marriage with Sally, for example, I realize that we weren't good at giving feedback, and eventually fell prey to destructive patterns of dealing (or not dealing) with conflict. My pattern was to angrily shut down disagreements. I'd often wade into the Danger Zone using sarcasm. Rather than becoming outwardly defensive, Sally tended to quickly withdraw.

I cringe recalling that once, with Sally eight months pregnant, as the light changed in the middle of us crossing a busy Chicago intersection, I cried out, "Can't you waddle any faster?!" That got a laugh from the friends who were with us. But Sally, already feeling self-conscious, wasn't smiling. She no doubt took my comment as demeaning. That's the problem with sarcasm. We think we're being funny, but most often we're just amusing ourselves in the Danger Zone. Over time, Sally became critical and contemptuous of me, and eventually withdrew permanently.

To avoid a long-term relationship meltdown, we need to consciously stay out of the Danger Zone—or catch ourselves quickly when we're there, take a deep breath, and make a different choice. First, recognize that any exchange you have with another person is an attempt by that person to connect with you in some way, and you have three choices in responding, what Gottman refers to as *Turning Against*, *Turning Away*, or *Turning Towards*.

Turning Against means you get angry or sarcastic, criticize the other person, exude contempt, and probably elicit a response of defensiveness or withdrawal. That's what I was inadvertently doing to Sally with my comment to her on the Chicago street. I recall another incident when I came home one evening from a particularly arduous day at the office and found Sally crying on the sofa, watching a re-run of the old TV western *Bonanza*. My sarcasm immediately kicked in, like "What the hell are you crying about? You know what kind of day I just had?!"

I unconsciously continued a *Turning Against* pattern in conflicts with Stacey, as I did in shutting down the conversations about having a child. She'd raise the issue, and I'd angrily raise all the reasons not to deal with it. *Turning Against* her wasn't a way of *having* conflict, but a way of *avoiding* it.

While consistently *Turning Against* will surely damage a relationship, *Turning Away* proves to be even more harmful in the long run. At least in *Turning Against*, we have some emotional connection. In *Turning Away*, we ignore a person or issue, whether consciously or inadvertently, and over time create a distance that weakens the relationship.

Turning Away happens when we're too afraid to confront someone, give feedback, or ask for what we need. When, after the Montana retreat, I avoided further conversations with Stacey about having a child, Stacey was reluctant to confront me. For several months, she did not continue to pursue this important need, until she realized that avoiding the issue would only build resentment, with consequences even worse than a difficult conversation.

Turning Away happens when you think you're too busy to stop and listen. Is the project you're working on—or the text message that just appeared—more important than giving your full attention to a conversation? *Turning Away* also happens when instead of actively listening to another person, you start telling your own story. When a spouse comes home from work after a tough day and starts to share their challenges, only for their partner to interrupt with their own lamentations—or outright change the subject—there's a missed opportunity for emotional connection, and distance creeps in instead.

Staying in this pattern of *Turning Against* and *Turning Away*, living in the Danger Zone, is like a salmon swimming upstream, relentlessly driven by unconscious behavior. When this behavior permeates a relationship, it leads to dysfunction, and people eventually stop trying. Resentment builds, the couple becomes more critical and contemptuous of each other, they lose their friendship, and the relationship turns belly up.

Fortunately, in the conflict Stacey and I experienced in deciding to have a child, she chose the *Siddhartha* way and consciously *engaged* me. She stopped ignoring the issue and got my attention, not by expressing anger, but by sharing her fear that not having a productive discussion would lead to eventual resentment and distance—which neither of us wanted. She clearly invoked *Siddhartha Principle One:* **ACCEPT. Meet yourself where you are, without judgment.** By being honest about her feelings, dropping the judgment that either one of us was inherently wrong, and sharing her fear, she helped me engage with her as well. We both met each other "where we were" and began the process of *Siddhartha Principle Two:* **LEARN. Find the lesson in your present challenge.**

We turned towards each other. In the case of "The Kid Issue," this meant engaging in the discussion over a long period of time. But just as with *Turning Against* or *Turning Away*, it's not how you deal with any one issue that's important. It's the *pattern* you create by the choices you make on a daily basis, one interaction at a time.

Turning Towards means stopping whatever you're doing to actively listen. It means giving your full attention—or arranging a better time to talk. You consciously stay out of the Danger Zone, and actively engage in difficult conversations, paving the way for the self-reflection and learning it takes to get something resolved.

Interestingly, Gottman's research indicates that most couple's conflicts actually *never* get resolved. My sense is, that's because many conflicts have roots that most people never address: differences in underlying values—what's truly important to one person but not the other—or emotional and behavioral habits that go back to childhood. What's even more important than resolving conflicts is how you treat each other while you're having it. Your relationship is more important than being right!

The *Siddhartha* method of having a productive conflict involves a 3-step approach to *consciously* engage: **Facts, Feelings, Request.**

First, establish a safe space. Ask your partner, "Is this a good time to talk?" If it isn't, don't start the conversation just because *you* want to. Make another appointment. Then use the 3 Steps:

1. **Share Facts**, in the form of a neutral observation. Explain the situation that is bothering you, keeping it brief and to the point. Choose your battles; don't use this as the time to bring up all your past grievances. Pay attention to your tone and body language, which will speak louder than anything you actually say.

2. **Share Feelings.** Next share how the above situation made you feel. Avoid sharing that you're "angry," as that's a secondary emotion. Usually hiding below anger is an emotion that your partner can more easily identify with, like hurt, sad, afraid, embarrassed. You're looking for connection and understanding.

3. **Make a Request.** Make a respectful and loving request—not a demand—that if the other person would consider doing, might help you feel better, resolve the issue, or avoid having the situation recur.

If you're on the *receiving* end, your job is simply to repeat back to your partner what you think you're hearing them say. This skill is known as a *Perception Check*. Do it frequently, at least at the end of each of the three steps above. While it may seem tedious or unnecessary, you may be amazed at how you have misunderstood or missed some important part of the communication.

A Perception Check also helps the Speaker be sure they are saying what they mean to say. Often, hearing the words played back can help the Speaker clarify their thoughts. As the Receiver, that's all you do. No retort, no counter-arguing, no shifting the blame. Just say "thank you." Allow time to sift what's true. You can come back later, preferably on a separate occasion as the Speaker in this 3-step process, *if resolution requires more than just an apology.*

Using this 3-step process, and being conscious of the Danger Zone, helps avoid an argument in the heat of the moment, especially if you've been triggered and you're experiencing some anger, fear or anxiety. Often, the situation is greatly diffused just by allowing the Speaker to be heard.

Applying the *Siddhartha Principles*, learning the skills of constructive conflict, keeping our relationship clear of things that are bothering us—and consciously sharing appreciations with each other—establishes a solid foundation for creating and maintaining a strong intimate relationship. *And* leads to some great "date time!" (You know, the ones you'll now be putting on your calendar.)

Not long ago on one of our dates, we pondered the question, "If we put up a billboard for you when you died, what would it say?" I came up with "He served the world well with his wisdom and kindness." I liked my wife's better: "For a good time, call Stacey."

Chapter 8: I'll Feel a Whole Lot Better

See, this too you have already learned from the water,
that it is good to strive downwards, to sink, to seek the depth.

I spied the triangular corner of a treasure chest poking from the beach. With effort, I put one bare foot ahead of the other, warm sand squishing through my toes. Bright rays of the sun glinted like stars on the rippled azure sea as gentle waves lapped the shore. The chest's darkened wood was cracked from age, trussed by rusted iron hinges. Approaching cautiously, excitedly, I kneeled. Then, with nervous anticipation, my hands dug away the sand, and lifting, I freed the heavy box from its resting place. The lock hung open. I removed it, set it gingerly on the sand, and paused with my fingertips cradling the lid's edge. I lifted the lid and looked inside. Here I discovered a faded parchment. Breaking the wax seal, I unfolded the paper to see one word revealed: **FORGIVENESS.**

Oh shit, I thought. *I don't really want to deal with that.*

I returned from this guided meditation, opening my eyes to the classroom at the University of Santa Monica (USM) where I sat with more than 250 students in the first weekend of a two-year master's program in Spiritual Psychology. We'd just taken this trip into our subconscious courtesy of the lead faculty, Mary and Ron Hulnick, who founded this program infusing the tools of psychology with spirituality to teach a powerful and practical approach to life mastery. The purpose of the group meditation was to discover the quality each of us individually needed to bring forward to resolve the most important issues in our present life—"issues" defined as anything disturbing our peace or remaining unhealed from our past.

More than a dozen years had passed since my divorce. I could see that, had it not been for the choices made by Sally and Tim, I may not have found Stacey, sold the company, moved to California, or had another child. As a result of the accompanying challenges, I forged a strong relationship with my adult children, and learned so much about myself. But deep down, I still believed that I'd been wronged. Anytime I thought about the affair, I felt angry and resentful. Now, through this guided meditation, my subconscious had presented me with an extraordinary challenge.

How could I forgive Sally and Tim, who had an affair behind my back for seven months, while my best friend Tim joined us on vacations? How could I possibly forgive these people who now lived in my former home, with my children, paying the bills with my former money? Sure, I was happier now. But wouldn't *forgiving* them mean I condoned what they'd done?

Granted, the whole experience had provided powerful motivation for me to learn what it takes to create and maintain a great relationship. I'd gained a lot from my work in therapy and read a library's worth of relationship books on my own. Ironically, it provided my next answer to the "So what do you *do*?" question. "Well, I run retreats to help couples build great relationships."

I started leading couples' retreats after a friend in the Young Presidents Organization asked me to do a presentation for their "forum," who met each month to support each other professionally and personally. Many of the issues raised by the group in each meeting concerned their marriages, and they knew I'd gained some expertise in applying principles of intimacy to my own life. A presentation to this group led to a weekend workshop with their spouses. Soon, I'd partnered with my friend Adelaide and launched a business of facilitating couples' retreats for members of the Young Presidents Organization, the Entrepreneurs Organization, and other groups dedicated to improving their relationships.

Through a friend, I learned of USM and applied to the master's program, hoping to gain more knowledge and credentials for use in my business. I remained a bit skeptical of the "spiritual" side of the program, being attracted more by the emphasis on practical application of psychology and "learning by doing" rather than academic theory.

Quite frankly, "God talk" made me uncomfortable. I'd associated it with fundamentalist judgments criticizing anyone from outside their belief system, and an attitude that "if you don't believe what I believe, you're going to hell." Nor was I convinced that the New Age style of spiritual practice served us better, since it sometimes seemed to be used as a "spiritual bypass" that overlooked practical changes we actually needed to make in our lives.

Turns out, USM wasn't selling either of those brands. Their curriculum utilizes methods developed by masters in the field of psychology over the past 50 years. Traditional psychological methods focus on resolving problems intellectually through logic, or at the emotional level by surfacing feelings we might have buried since childhood, or behaviorally by redirecting us to act in healthier ways. USM's "spiritual" psychology leverages these three approaches to explore a deeper layer, uncovering the negative judgments we hold against ourselves or others, and moving into forgiveness, opening the door to compassion and love (the core of one's spiritual self).

When I use the term "judgment" in this context, I'm referring to the tendency we have to brand other people as wrong or bad. Judgments often arise because we think that people should be different than they are. In other words, we have formed some belief or standard that defines "the way they ought to be." And when a person violates that standard, we get triggered emotionally, experiencing anger, sadness, or fear.

There is a difference between judging a person and evaluating their actions or choices. I might disagree with their choice of behavior, especially if I observe that it brings harm to others, but my evaluation of their behavior can be clouded by my entering into judgment that they are inherently a "bad" person. Evaluation is simply determining effectiveness in the process of making decisions. For example, if I were hiring someone for a job that required tremendous initiative, it would affect my evaluation to learn that the applicant spent the last five years without a job, mostly watching TV and playing video games. I might evaluate that this person has not clearly demonstrated initiative based on their choices over the last five years (and I might be inaccurate). But I would clearly slip into *judgment* if I labeled the person as lazy, unambitious or worthless, as if it were the permanent state of their fundamental character.

Another reason to stay out of the murky waters of judgment is because in the short term, it's impossible to determine whether events in our life are "good" or "bad." Those people we regard as bringing harm may in fact, in the long run, have brought us a gift instead.

There's a parable that speaks to the fallacy of judgments: One day, a farmer's prized stallion breaks out of the corral and runs away. All the neighbors lament how terrible that is. The farmer just says, "Who's to say, good or bad?" The next day, the stallion returns with a bevy of mares. The neighbors rejoice, "How wonderful!" The farmer replies, "Who's to say, good or bad?" Later that week, the farmer's son rides the stallion, falls off and breaks his leg. The neighbors say, "How unfortunate, how awful!" The farmer says, "Who's to say, good or bad?" The following day, the army marches through town conscripting all the young men in the village to go to war. They pass over the farmer's injured boy. Good or bad, who's to say?

Initial judgments can prove to be flawed. Further, when we engage in negative judgments, we experience distressing emotions—upset, anger, sadness. Often, instead of taking responsibility for our own upset and examining what might be faulty about our assumptions, we blame others for our pain. Without realizing it, we cast ourselves as victims. Then, we become highly critical and contemptuous of others. That behavior, in turn, begets a negative reaction from them. This fuels our judgments even more. And so the vicious cycle continues.

To make matters worse, below the surface lie even more complex challenges. What will often fuel our judgment of others are the unrecognized judgments we make against *ourselves*, known in psychology as *projections*. Long ago in business, I came across an adage that every time we point a finger at someone, three more point back at us. Now I realize that those fingers represent three types of projections:

1. How the behaviors we object to in others are actually the same ones we engage in ourselves;

2. How we often treat *ourselves* the same way we criticize *others* for treating us; and

3. How we see "life," the universe, or God to be mistreating us.

For example, if I'm upset that someone betrayed me, it's easier to blame my betrayer than to examine how I may have betrayed *him* or *her* in some way, how I may have betrayed *myself* by not staying true to my values, or how I feel betrayed or unlovable by God (or some higher power), or by the world—which is a misperception that allows me to maintain my status as a victim.

When we get stuck in a cycle of projections, we have difficulty escaping self-righteousness, anger, and pain. To get unstuck, we must clearly identify the judgments that lurk below our irrational beliefs, our emotional upsets, or our dysfunctional behaviors. To accomplish this goal, in effect we have to remove our perceptual filters, like taking off a pair of tinted glasses. Doing so, we can begin to see things differently, find different ways to "hold" our experiences, and change our interpretations of events.

For example, if I'm upset that someone betrayed me, I could instead see events through their eyes and try to understand their perception. I can accept that their "take" on the experience is just as valid as mine.

But recognizing judgments against ourselves and others isn't the same as releasing them. So, what's the path to inner peace? Forgiveness.

Forgiveness means that we let go of the judgments we've been holding about others. The reason we should let them go is that judgments fuel an inner disturbance. And since judgments are based on beliefs that may not be true anyway, why are we making ourselves upset by hanging onto them? Even if our perception of past events is accurate, we can recognize that people do the best they know how—or they'd be doing something better or more effective. Letting go of our judgments is a crucial first step on the path to experiencing greater inner peace.

When I first signed up for the master's program, my goal was to learn tools I could use to help others. Little did I realize I'd be practicing them on myself. I stood at the threshold of a new level of consciousness about my life. Siddhartha stirred.

☙

*That I know nothing about myself, that Siddhartha has stayed
so foreign and unfamiliar to me, comes from one cause, solely one:
I was afraid of me, I was on the run from myself!*

I was flying in the cockpit of a four-engine plane, observing the pilots. No one spoke. The pilots knew where we were going, but I had no idea. The scene shifted, and simultaneously I was sitting at a conference table on the top floor of a multi-story building rising above the middle of the ocean. Its foundation rested on the ocean floor. I was surrounded by officers dressed in khaki uniforms, and I realized I was in the "war room." Suddenly, I was back in the airplane, shocked and panicked by the realization that our mission was to attack the building I was simultaneously sitting in. The pilots pushed the wheel forward, and down we went into the ocean, deeper and deeper, finally crashing into the building's foundation at the bottom of the sea. The explosion rocked the building I was in. It began to collapse. And I woke up, shaken.

It was 6 a.m. on the Monday after my first class weekend at USM. The message of the nightmare was clear: The work I was doing would shake me to the core. Ultimately, it would destroy many of my long-held beliefs, reveal the illusions that had clouded my perception of reality, and tear open old wounds that had been hastily stitched together to hide weakness and fear. Step by step, I would examine the very foundations of my life. Unearth my limiting beliefs. Reveal my negative judgments. Shine light on the dark places I'd hidden inside.

In the first year of the masters program, I revisited the dynamics of my first marriage, reliving the divorce war, and examining my part in it. I dug deep into the pain, the betrayal, the beliefs about how it "should" have been, the losses, and the resentments. I struggled with forgiving Sally and Tim. While I understood the theory of judgments and forgiveness, it sure wasn't easy to put it into practice. Ultimately, the invitation to forgive others would cause me to explore my childhood, examining the walls I'd constructed around my own emotions, the ways I'd learned to avoid healthy conflict and speaking up for myself, the patterns I'd carried into my first marriage and lugged along with me still.

My breakthroughs didn't come in one spectacular moment, but slowly over many months. The process was like peeling away the skin of an onion. As I examined one layer of my experience and addressed the accompanying judgments, beliefs and perceptions, a new, even deeper layer would emerge. The abandonment by my wife and best friend dredged up all the feelings of abandonment throughout my life and focused them like rays of sun through a magnifying glass. As a kid, I'd used a glass like that to fry ants. Metaphorically, as an adult, I used that hot energy to rage my way through the divorce, trying to fry Sally and Tim. Now it was time to use the magnifying glass in a different way, to examine myself and how I held my experiences.

What a shock I had, realizing that through my marriage, I had reproduced the dynamics of my own childhood! With Sally I had unwittingly recreated my childhood feelings of emotional abandonment, a lack of intimacy, and my conditioned pattern of avoiding conflict. I'd expected both Sally and myself to play the same game I'd witnessed with my parents: The dutiful, self-sacrificing, never-complaining wife raising the children while the husband, the martyr, fought the corporate battles for Truth, Justice and the American Way.

Meanwhile, if Sally had stepped into the fairy tale of being carried off by the prince to live happily ever after, life in the Chicago suburbs with the King of Rust-Oleum wasn't quite Camelot. Sally became miserable, repelled by the role of "corporate wife," feeling shut down, dominated and controlled by me. The kingdom imploded. Tim arrived to rescue Sally from the Castle of Doom.

Reflecting back on Tim's life at the time, he was in the middle of a difficult divorce. Perhaps out of a shared sense of loneliness, their affair began. Sally was probably desperate for affection, and both of them longed to escape. Given the circumstances, in hindsight, their choices were not so surprising.

Of course, this is all just conjecture on my part. I don't know what Sally and Tim were thinking at the time, what truly motivated them. I was just shifting my perspective to try to see through their eyes, feel through their hearts, reaching for a place of empathy and compassion.

Looking back, I realized I might have gone on for years in that marriage, with the belief that I could fix any problem, and I would never have allowed myself to "fail" by having a divorce. I have a hard time comprehending how I ever would have moved on, or found real happiness. Not long before my marriage imploded, I had felt the uneasiness in my heart. *I've reached the top of my career, I'm president of the company, I have a big house and two great children*, I thought. *But is this all there is?* I yearned to live in a warmer climate, wanted to travel the world, and longed to feel *alive* in my marriage. Yet I had no idea how I could possibly change my life. The cards were dealt. I'm all in. Keep swimming.

So, what a gift Sally and Tim unwittingly gave me! The divorce provided intense motivation to look at myself, understand my blind spots, and learn the meaning and value of emotional intimacy. Oddly enough, it made possible my wildest dreams. At the same time, Tim and Sally gave each other gifts. They've been married now for longer than Sally and I were together, so their "affair" wasn't just a fleeting escape, but a long term relationship. What they did wasn't *against* me. It was for themselves.

Could they have made those self-honoring choices in a way that didn't bring me so much pain? Maybe. Maybe not. The human mind acts on what it perceives as reality. Maybe in Sally's eyes, I was self-centered and obsessed with my business. Perhaps I'd damaged her self-esteem. And it would be understandable if she felt justified to hurt me back. What if Sally and Tim just fell in love, and didn't know how to break the news? Perhaps they feared my reaction, were confused about what to do, or were thrilled by a clandestine affair that made them both feel alive. In any case, they did what they did. It got them both to where they wanted to be. Ironically, it eventually got me to where I wanted to be, too.

We all did the best we knew at the time, given our perceptions, skills, fears, insecurities, and the sum total of our life experiences. If we'd known how to do it differently, we would have. With this new awareness, I gained compassion for us all. We all get through this life the best we can, and lots of times it's pretty messy. That time, we all learned through pain rather than through wisdom.

By forgiving, I didn't condone their behavior, but accepted the humanness in each of us. In fact, my last obstacle in forgiving Sally and Tim proved the hardest: Forgiving *myself*. Releasing them from culpability left me to accept my own responsibility for contributing to the breakdown of the marriage, for the anger I expressed through our divorce, for my own pattern of conflict avoidance. I painfully recognized that by casting judgment against Sally for abandoning me, I'd failed to see how I had been abandoning *myself*. Through my marriage, I'd buried my true feelings. Through my divorce, I nearly buried my true self.

Do I judge and blame myself? Or do I forgive myself for doing the best I knew how at the time? This hit home: Life is a school for learning, and we each come with our own curriculum. Some of our teachers might slap us with rulers just to get our attention; others act like Mother Teresa. Either way, what really matters is what we *learn* from our experiences. I forgave myself for judging that I should have been any different than I was. I learned this: Forgiveness earns an "A." And the "A" stands for Acceptance. That's part of what gave Siddhartha a peaceful smile, and helped me feel a whole lot better.

I have learned through my body and my soul that I much
needed sin; I needed lust, the pursuit of possessions, vanity;
and I needed the most humiliating desperation in order to learn
how to give up resistance, in order to learn how to love the
world, and no longer to compare it to some world wished,
imagined by me, to a kind of perfection as contrived by me, but
to leave it as it is, and to love it, and to gladly be a part of it.

Chapter 9: Here Comes the Sun

But all I care about is to be able to love the world,
not to despise it, not to hate it and myself, to be able to regard it
and me and all beings with love and admiration and reverence.

Near the end of the first year at USM, I shared some of my new insights on a hike with my daughter—and my forgiveness of Tim and her mom. Tears of joy welled in her eyes. We stopped walking, looked at each other, and she gave me a big hug. I could almost see some invisible weight lift from her. She shared how hard it had been to feel caught in between her mother and me, through all the years of verbal sparring and silent seething.

"I know this will mean a lot to my brother, too," she said, with a smile of relief.

Wow! I got to feel better in two ways, unburdening myself *and* having a positive impact on my children. Ironically, withholding acceptance had been working against my desire for greater closeness with my children. The alchemy of forgiveness transformed my hardened heart of steel into priceless gold.

Soon afterward, on the occasion of my daughter's graduation from college, I asked Sally and Tim to meet with me. The morning before the commencement ceremony, we got together at a Starbucks. We could all have used more than strong coffee.

"I just want to apologize for all the anger I sent your way through the divorce and ever since," I began. "I want you to know I hold no ill feelings towards either of you. I've come to realize that if you didn't do what you did, in exactly the way you did it, I wouldn't have learned some important lessons, and I wouldn't be where I am today, which is a very happy place. So, what I thought at the time was so horrible actually turned out to be a gift. I'm sorry it took me so long to realize that."

Surprising both myself and them, I added, "I want to thank you, too, for being a great mother and step-dad to our children."

Holding back tears, Sally agreed, "Yes, our children are pretty wonderful, aren't they?" She may have been deflecting my sincere compliment, as well as the forgiveness and apology, but that was OK. This was more for me than for either of them.

Tim, too, said little, his face frozen in reflective silence. Was he dumbfounded? Did he distrust my motive? Then, afterward, he took me aside. "You know, Don, I still struggle with feeling guilty about what I did."

"Well, Tim, I encourage you to do whatever you have to do to release that," I replied sincerely. "I have no animosity towards you, and I have no intention of making you feel guilty. So, it's really your choice to hold onto it or let it go. I hope, for your sake, you can let it go."

My daughter has since told me she dreaded ever having a wedding because she couldn't imagine her father and mother in the same room together. Now she can…because she's actually experienced it. As I write this, she's happily married and has a family of her own!

Through the weeks and months that spanned my two years at USM, I would discover that acceptance didn't apply just to Sally and Tim. I would uncover subconscious judgments I held about my parents. I would trace back my feelings of abandonment to the unexpressed resentment I had towards my dad for dying so suddenly. In moving towards acceptance, I recognized the gift in my father's early death—his example to me about not taking life for granted, and his freeing me to make my own decisions at Rust-Oleum, including the eventual sale of the company.

I longed to talk with my father, to share my feelings, and to know what he might say in reply. Since he was no longer alive for a conversation in person, I decided to write him a letter:

Dad, thank you for supporting me in everything I did, for encouraging the best in me. Your humility and honesty remain gifts in my heart. Thank you for the foundation you laid at Rust-Oleum, for all your years of hard work and struggle. I know you hung in there not just for yourself, but for me. I did the best I knew how, to make you proud. I forgive you for leaving me so early; I know it was your time to move on. You didn't need a blue ribbon to know you'd left a job well done. I love you.

I applied a psychological technique known as a "Gestalt" strategy to create an internal dialogue with my father. I wasn't really communicating with the dead, simply working to resolve some old unfinished business between my father and myself. I imagined a "letter" in reply, and simply wrote what came to me:

Don, I knew you had everything it took to carry on the company. It would have been tough for me to part with Rust-Oleum, and it was up to your generation to make that decision, and my time to move on. Thank you for carrying on the Fergusson tradition of perseverance, courage and humility. I'm glad you broke the family pattern of endless work and an early heart attack. I had once hoped to retire at 40, so I'm glad you took the opportunity yourself. Take the time to enjoy your life, and don't take a moment for granted. I'm beaming with pride. Your grandfather is proud, too. Be at peace.

How do I know that's what my dad would have said? I don't. But that's what bubbled up in my consciousness when I asked. The real payoff came in healing my inner relationship with my father. I released beliefs that no longer served me, and recognized the unconscious judgments I had held against myself and my father.

I had work to do with my grandfather, too, though I'd never met him. I used the same strategy and wrote the Captain a letter:

Grand-dad, I still carry a burden in my heart that I have let you down by selling the company. I remember seeing a letter you wrote before your death, saying, "This company will never be sold by me or future generations." Somehow I knew, when I came into the company, that the decision to keep it or sell it would fall on my shoulders. To this day, I don't know if I did the right thing; whether I decided to sell because I was exhausted from fighting the battle, from a place of weakness. Or if I was in touch with my true self, the place deep inside that knew the time was right—for myself, my family, and the future of the company. I've lost count of the number of times I've questioned myself about whether I did the right thing to part with our family heritage. Each time, in my mind, I go back through the situation I faced and what I knew at the time. And each time, I come to the same conclusion. I also look at the life I've created since that time—the life I wouldn't have had if I stayed at Rust-Oleum. And I shudder to think what I would have missed. So why can't I unburden my heart?

And in my imagination that tough old Scotsman replied:

Donnie-boy, laddie, when I wrote that letter about never selling the company, I saw Rust-Oleum on the threshold of becomin' something. It was the ticket out of the sufferin' and poverty that generations of my family had endured. I didn't want any son o' mine—or grandson—to part with it lightly. And you didn't. We each played our part, laddie, and we each lived the life we chose to live. You came into this world with a great heritage and a great obligation. You lived up to it.

You see, the important thing wasn't to carry on the company—it's just a "thing" which will one day pass away just like each of us. You have the opportunity now to enjoy life in a way I couldn't, me boys couldn't. And because you sold the business, you've created for yourself the opportunity to help the lives of others a whole lot more than keeping the rust away. You see, you really don't know how the story ends, do you? Haven't you learned, as you look back on your life, not to judge where you are in the moment, simply to live your life as it presents itself—and have a little faith?

Live like you're me, Donnie-boy. How do you know you aren't? Don't you think if I could've come back as you, I would've? After all, I had some things to learn about being betrayed—don't forget, my first mate ran off with my first wife! Served him right, the scallywag! But if he hadn't, I wouldn't have had two sons to carry on the business, and you wouldn't have been born. Sound familiar? I also had a thing or two to learn about livin' the hard life, and learnin' to love.

You haven't sold the heritage, laddie, you're just writing the next chapter.

By writing my letter to the Captain, and imagining his reply, I realized that the company had been a means to teach me self-trust, interdependence, and the meaning of accountability. These were the true gifts—not shares of stock—that I could carry through my life. In imagining that the Captain held no judgments against me for selling the company, I could forgive my own self-judgments, and move on.

What he had said to Gotama: that his, the Buddha's, treasure was not the teaching, but the unspeakable and unteachable that he had once experienced in the hour of his enlightenment—this was precisely what he now set forth to experience, what he now began to experience. He had now to experience himself.

I was sitting in a room with nearly 200 fellow students, a week before graduating from USM, during the last days of an intensive week-long practicum. We'd just completed two years of deep spiritual exploration with thousands of hours of counseling and therapeutic practice. The program faculty issued a challenge: dive deeper into your relationship with the Divine. We began a free-form meditation. I set a bold intention: to know Spirit.

I closed my eyes, took a few deep breaths, and cleared my mind. Time passed, and I sunk deeper. Suddenly, I felt electricity coursing through my brain. I had the sensation of being lifted physically, then accelerating to light speed. My inner awareness burst through an invisible boundary separating my current life from a place beyond it.

As if watching a rapid-fire movie, I saw all the people and experiences of my life spread out before me in an endless line, a tunnel from the present to the past. I realized I could reframe every event just by flipping a switch in my mind. Click, click, click, a thousand times. I didn't change the experiences; I changed how I held them. Suddenly, I realized that everything in my life had been provided to me for my learning, growth and spiritual evolution. All of it came from a place of love, for my highest good. I didn't just think this, I *knew* it.

In this place, judgment did not exist. It wasn't a matter of *not having* judgments or releasing them—they didn't even *exist*, like air in outer space. I held myself in this place for as long as I could, the top of my head feeling as if it were engulfed in an electrical storm. Finally, I got a little freaked out. That's as close to "knowing God" as I could handle that day.

I returned my awareness to the room, back to my breath, back to my body, back in my chair, sitting in that room with 200 people who had all become supportive friends helping each other find their own way from Salmon to Siddhartha. I thought I'd just glimpsed the path.

Now, I'm not saying I'd found Truth with a capital "T," nor become Enlightened. Perhaps there is no God. Maybe we all just die, get eaten by worms, and that's that. But I've now adopted a philosophy that gives me inspiration and hope, helps me make sense of my life, supports me in being more loving, and is grounded in my own experience and reality.

After the practicum, I made one more important transformation in my relationship with Sally and Tim: I went beyond forgiveness to love. I saw clearly how our paths had intertwined, that it was all as it should be, and I loved them for the role they'd played in deepening my life's learning. That didn't mean I had to like them, or make them my best friends. And maybe, in the shift from judgment and resentment to gratitude and love, I'd just freed myself from having to play another round of the betrayal and drama game in the future. I'd learned an important lesson this time, and didn't need to experience another marriage betrayal to reveal my own self-betrayal.

Here's what I've discovered about the path from forgiveness to love. We must recognize that we are all doing the best we know how—or else we'd be doing it differently. When we forgive ourselves for judging ourselves or others, we shift from our heads to our hearts. In our hearts, we find compassion and love. So, when we shift from judgment to forgiveness, we discover a place where the true spirit within each of us connects with the greater Spirit.

My purpose in sharing these ideas is not to dissuade anyone from their own particular religious or spiritual beliefs. I don't pretend to know how the Universe works. It just seems to me that this perspective does no harm, creates a better world around me, and inspires me to live my best (and happiest) life.

But what a journey this was! I had to go through so much foolishness, so much vice, so much error, so much disgust and disappointment and misery, only to become a child again and to be able to begin anew...where else may my journey lead me?

Although I worked hard to release judgments about other people, I still had some lingering self-judgments. Since the time I was 16 and I started working at Rust-Oleum, I'd been more of a human *doing* than a human *being*. In fact, I'd been so driven by the self-imposed obligation to accomplish—to do more—I'd forgotten how to just *be*. Deep down, despite all my achievements, I'd never felt *good enough*. So I tried to overcome that feeling by being a perfectionist—which, of course, kept me stuck in the circle of never feeling good enough, because of course, I could never be perfect!

I still hadn't found the answer to the question, "So what do you *do*?" and thought if only I could find that answer, I'd feel better. At first, I thought the answer came in becoming a motivational speaker and seminar leader. That would be respectable.

But wait a minute, I thought to myself. Would that really make me happy? Do I really want to travel like that? That's just what I think I should do. If I really want to feel happy, I'd be like...Jimmy Buffett! I laughed out loud. *Yeah, I thought, Jimmy Buffett plays music and clearly has fun doing it. He flies floatplanes, sails, surfs, and fishes. He writes books. He even started his own Margaritaville restaurants. And he did that just at the time he thought his career was winding down!*

I considered the ways I resembled this idol. I loved music and writing. I enjoyed sailing, windsurfing, skeet shooting, and fishing, though I'd left those behind for more "purposeful" pursuits. I had a sense of humor, often buried under the weight of seriousness. Indeed, like this exalted personality, my life resembled more patchwork than precision. To paraphrase one of Jimmy's song titles, I was growing older but not up, resisting a simple answer to the question, "So what do you *do*?" And nothing's wrong with that!

Right then and there, I made a "contract" with myself:

I hereby release myself of the burden that I'm not good enough and need to prove myself. And I give myself permission to enjoy my life and success, and experience Love & Joy!

Of course, just writing the contract didn't make it so. Action must follow intention—Siddhartha Principle Four: **ACT. Take small steps every day to create your desired experience.** I consciously set aside any consideration of what I'd do for "work" or career, entering what I called "The Gap," a sort of sabbatical where I'd create space to discover what made my heart sing. I realized something important: Finding joy isn't an intellectual process, but an *experiential* one. We find out what we love by directly experimenting with new roles in life.

We don't have to quit our jobs to discover what would bring us greater joy in our lives. A thoughtful walk on the beach, a stroll through the forest, quiet meditation time in the morning, a heartfelt conversation with a person you trust, a short-term evening class at a local college—any of these could help provide answers.

Whatever path you choose, the journey begins with setting an intention. For example, I set an intention in "The Gap" to learn to sail, play the guitar, or try something new without judging myself. Next, take a very small, manageable step to actually *experience* what it is you think you'd love. You don't have to jump in with both feet. Instead, just *lean into* it. I've found that if I am really in alignment with a new path, doors will open. If I find myself having to bash through immoveable barriers, perhaps there's another way in; or maybe it's just not the right path.

The key is to listen to your heart, knowing that whatever you choose, the real gain will come not just from what you do but from what you learn about yourself in the process of doing. This certainly proved true as I leaned into my first project in "The Gap." Years ago, I'd enjoyed the feeling of freedom as a 15-knot breeze powered my little Sunfish across a bay, and how exhilarated I'd felt after then sailing a 40-foot Jeanneau. I realized sailing was my perfect metaphor for practicing *being* rather than doing. It put me in the moment, challenged me literally to "go with the flow," connected me with Nature and my own spirit, and built confidence and self-esteem, without any "productive" outcome other than enjoyment itself. I took five sailing courses, one evolving naturally to the next, with the intention to gain sufficient mastery to allow me to sail a 50-foot boat virtually anywhere in the world. In the process, I found myself learning more than just captaining a boat: I had to face my fears of making mistakes, my need to be perfect, and my feelings of being "not good enough."

After learning to sail, I reflected on an "Ideal Scene" I'd created years earlier, my vision of how I wanted my life to be in the future: *I am feeling thrilled by the adventure of sailing with Stacey to the Channel Islands, sighting pods of dolphin and whales.* At that time, I had no idea how I'd make it come true. I first utilized *Siddhartha Principle Three:* **CLARIFY. Create an ideal scene of your desired experience.** Then employing

Siddhartha Principle Four, not fighting my way to these goals, but taking small steps in the direction of my dream, I allowed it to come to me in due time.

With sailing now in my life, I pondered what other dreams I'd denied myself. I looked back on other Ideal Scenes I'd written years earlier: *I am having great fun creating beautiful music with Stacey, playing drums and bass guitar, joyfully jamming with friends, and enjoying occasional gigs at local clubs.* At the time I wrote those statements, I didn't own a drum set, have the foggiest idea how to play a bass guitar, nor did I know any musicians.

In deciding to lean into this Ideal Scene, I took the initial steps of buying my dream DW drum set and a bass guitar. From there, doors opened, and all I had to do was pay attention. In casual conversation with my first sailing instructor, Jon Payne, I learned he was an avid guitarist. He mentioned that the Director of the Sailing Center, who had arranged my sailing courses, was once the bassist in his old band. Both were excited to have a drummer (me) to jam with. My dry cleaner gave me the lead for a guitar teacher to get me started on bass, when I happened to mention my interest in music. Then, a musical equipment problem led me to seek out the manager of a local guitar shop. He not only fixed the problem, but joined in our musical jam sessions and planted the seed that sprouted what seemed like a crazy mid-life decision, to form our first band and take a wild ride to Abbey Road Studios and The Cavern Club.

As Stacey and I leaned into this first musical project, the *Siddhartha Principles* emerged.

Chapter 10: One Ride

I commend you, Siddhartha: after so many years of foolishness, you once again have had an idea, you have done something, you have heard the bird in your heart sing and followed it!

It was drizzling cool rain just after noon as the five of us dropped our bags at the newly opened Hard Days Night Hotel in Liverpool, England. We were exhausted from traveling, and we had only an hour before we were due on stage at The Cavern Club. My bandmates headed over to set up. I was suddenly regretting my decision, made just six months earlier, to play bass guitar in a rock band with my wife, and travel to Liverpool to play at a club made famous by the Beatles.

In the lobby, my wife and I were surrounded by Beatles photos on the wall, and "All You Need Is Love" played in the background. We were going to need a lot more than love to pull this thing off. My stomach churned from nervous energy. Our rooms weren't ready.

"Where's the restroom?" my wife and lead singer Stacey asked, panic in her eyes. "I've got to change clothes and do my make-up. My hair looks like shit." She left abruptly.

I found the men's room at the hotel, splashed water on my face, and changed out of my travel-weary clothes, pulling on a black t-shirt, black jeans, and a black leather vest from my small duffle bag. I felt surprisingly good, considering we got back after midnight from recording our first original song at Abbey Road Studios, celebrated with a couple of nightcaps, woke up to catch a 6 a.m. car to Heathrow airport for our flight to Manchester, caught the train to Liverpool's Lime Street Station, and then hailed the taxi that brought us here. I was amazed we'd actually made it.

Pacing the lobby waiting for Stacey, I pretended to busy myself looking at old photos on the wall of John Lennon, Paul McCartney, George Harrison, and Ringo Starr. I silently repeated an affirmation:

I am calm, confident, and poised.
I am positively energized and clearly focused.
I am easily remembering my bass lines.
I am gracefully accurate and abundantly joyful.

Crap. I just hoped I wouldn't totally blank out on stage. Where was Stacey? *OK, calm down,* I thought. We still had 20 minutes. She appeared.

"Ready?" I asked.

"I can't do this!" Stacey replied, panicked.

"Breathe with me," I said, locking my eyes into hers. "Repeat after me: 'I am calm, confident, and poised...'"

"Yeah right, let's go," she said.

The drizzle had turned to downpour as we passed beneath the neon sign proclaiming *The Cavern Club.* Down, down we spiraled on the narrow stairs. Entering the dimly lit pub, I was surprised to find so many people huddled at wooden tables on that early Sunday afternoon, loudly talking and laughing under the low brick arches, pints of stout and cocktails already half consumed. "Wow, nice crowd," I yelled at Stacey, trying to be heard above the din of a local band blasting the Beatles' song, "Help!" They sounded really good.

Ohmygod, I thought. *What am I doing here?*

The tribute band hit their final note and then I heard, "Thanks, everybody. Now stay put for the next band, all the way from Santa Barbara, California...The Ride!"

Minutes later, ready or not, showtime! Our guitarists ripped into the opening riff of "All Shook Up," and before Stacey could finish "Bless my soul, what's wrong with me," I felt drops of sweat streaming off my brow. We nailed the first song. Cheers from the audience, and a crowd off the street streamed down the stairs into The Cavern. I glanced over at our drummer, tucked into the back corner of the stage, guitar amps in front of him on either side. He leaned towards me and mouthed, "I can't hear a thing!" Then, he rapped his sticks together to count us in, one—two—three—four, and we launched the next song. Guitars hit the opening chords in unison, Stacey wailed on harmonica, and the drummer played by feel. I looked up from the fretboard, squinting through the spotlights at the gyrating crowd. My ears deafened as "I Should Have Known Better" echoed off the low ceiling. I imagined the Beatles there. I grinned big. I was playing The Cavern Club! My mind's eye snapped a photo, and the little kid in me took it all in, breathless. Then, as Stacey sang the bridge, I lost my place and played an E instead of a B. I just grinned bigger, regained my fingering, and moved on.

It's not a dream if you choose to make it your ride.

—Stacey & Don Fergusson, "One Ride"

For Christmas before my 12th birthday, I got my first two record albums: *Meet the Beatles* and their latest, *Beatles '65*. Soon afterward, I started taking drum lessons, and for my birthday that February, my parents bought me a set of blue-sparkle Ludwigs.

Through my teens, I drummed along to my favorite songs, cranked up full blast on a cheap record player in my basement. All the vibration made the needle hop around so much that I finally taped a nickel to the tone arm to drag it through the vinyl grooves. I practiced the rudiments and mimicked the beats I heard on the records, from Ringo to Led Zeppelin's John Bonham.

A few friends took guitar lessons back then, but none played well enough to form a band. Drums dropped out of my life when I went to college. Then, it was time to get serious working in the family business. It would be 30 years before I'd give myself permission to own another set. And little did I know what doors would open as I leaned into something just for fun: learning to play bass guitar.

After graduating from USM, I decided to take a year-long sabbatical and give myself permission to play music. I found a guitar teacher to work with me on bass, and the journey began. Shortly after I began earnestly plucking at the bass guitar, a local musician,

David, handed me a flyer for Main Stage Dream Tours: "Here's your chance to form a rock band, record at Abbey Road Studios, and play the famous Cavern Club in Liverpool, England," he explained. "My drummer and I have all the contacts in the UK to make it happen."

"That sounds great," I replied. "I'd love to do that someday, after I learn what I'm doing on bass guitar."

David called me the next month for a jam session, just for fun. And I agreed, just for fun. We hit it off, though I could hardly play that bass. I invited our guitarist friend Jon to join in, and Stacey strummed a few chords on rhythm guitar and played tambourine.

After our second session, David said, "Well, what about it? You guys should sign up for the Dream Tour in June. We've got tickets guaranteed for the Paul McCartney concert in Liverpool. It's a once-in-a-lifetime chance." Then he turned to Stacey, "Can you sing?"

"Who, me?" Stacey replied, shocked. "No. I can play tambourine. Better yet, I'll just film the performance."

"But you've always wanted to sing, Stacey," I said matter-of-factly, even though I knew she was terrified of even *speaking* in front of a crowd. "And I could probably be ready by then with a few songs on bass, and play the rest of them on drums."

"No way," Stacey said. "I'd make a complete fool of myself. I can't sing."

Jon, a 20-year veteran of several rock bands, put his arm around my shoulder and gingerly asked, "Have you guys ever *done* a live gig before?"

"Well, no…" I stammered. Then I smiled, "So what's your point?"

Stacey and I went to bed that night letting go of the dream. A little too crazy, a little too soon. "Perhaps someday," we told each other.

But the next morning, Stacey had changed her mind: "I was up half the night thinking about this, Don," she confided. "This is the opportunity of a lifetime. I'm not going to let fear stand in the way of doing something I've always wanted to do. I'm going to sing!"

"You are?" I said, shocked.

"Yes. And you're going to play bass guitar!" she added.

"I am?"

"That's right," Stacey said. "Someday is today."

We had less than six months to learn an hour-long set of music to be played at The Cavern Club in Liverpool. I'd already been working for two months on one Beatles song, "I Should Have Known Better," and still couldn't get through it without screwing up. We also had to write an original song to be recorded at Abbey Road Studios in London. And no, I'd never written a song before. I also needed to find an actual bass teacher, and Stacey needed to learn how to sing. Other than that, no worries, mate!

The Salmon leapt upstream, struggling along and hitting boulders, as an old program of pessimistic and limiting beliefs kicked in. *I'm not good enough to do this. I'll need to learn five years of music theory in the next six months. Only if I can play complicated bass lines will it prove I have talent. I'll never find the time to practice. And what makes me think I can write a song? Even if I could, I still can't play it! Besides, is music worth spending all this time and money on just for my own enjoyment? Am I being selfish, and just making a fool of myself?*

I jumped on the Internet and printed out sheet music for the songs we were considering. I searched online for bass lessons, printed out pages of scales and riffs, bought a copy of *Bass Guitar for Dummies*, and ordered some equipment for an in-home studio.

I felt as if I had just joined the Olympics gymnastics squad and couldn't yet hold a handstand. Could I even *do* this in six months? All I knew was, I couldn't do it at that moment. If it's only rock and roll, why did I feel such PANIC!

Facing despair, I fell back into the river, feeling the current flowing hard against me. I realized that to reach the surface and breathe again, I needed to get back in touch with my original intention. I had stepped into this for fun, learning, the enjoyment of playing in a band, and the rich experience that would come from a once-in-a-lifetime opportunity to perform at The Cavern Club. But now, I was creating pressure on myself by imposing an arbitrary standard of where I thought I was *supposed* to be.

With this fresh self-awareness (and perhaps a bit of desperation), I discovered *Siddhartha Principle One*: **ACCEPT. Meet yourself where you are, without judgment.**

On this journey of playing bass guitar, that meant accepting my current capabilities. What if I stopped thinking of myself as a fraud and just acknowledged that I was a novice? What if I really *didn't* have to learn five years of music theory just to play 10 songs? Hey, what if it didn't matter at all what the audience thought, as long as I had a good time?

To put that principle into practice, the first step involved simplifying the bass lines to something I could play *now*. I let go of the idea that it had to be complicated to be good, or to make *me* feel good enough. When I'd mastered a simple version, I added a few more riffs I could manage without stressing out. To put it another way, I made friends with my fingers instead of cursing their inability to get it right.

Still, the clock was ticking and I was a long way from even playing simple versions of the songs in the set list, much less writing an original song. Instead of breathing easier, I continued to spiral downward through the eddies and into the muck.

Here's what I found down there: that deep and familiar feeling that I wasn't good enough which appears when I feel most overwhelmed. Again! I felt it as a kid, when I knew everyone expected me to take over the family business. I felt it fresh out of business school, taking the helm of a leaky corporate ship on an unsettled sea. A failed marriage lent yet more evidence for the case against myself. And despite all the work I'd done to expunge these limiting beliefs, here they rise again, like the Creature from the Black Lagoon.

Swimming like a salmon wouldn't end this horror flick. I had to operate like Siddhartha, relying on *Siddhartha Principle Two*: **LEARN. Find the lesson in your present challenge.**

I realized that the Creature from the Black Lagoon bore a gift—an opportunity to heal a long-held, self-imposed wound that I wasn't good enough. My lesson from this challenge was that the belief "I'm not good enough" was always irrational. I was just never good enough for *me*.

Rather than rage against myself for what I saw as the re-emergence of a weakness, I could acknowledge myself for how far I'd come. It was precisely because I had gained greater self-awareness that I could see the old pattern at work and make a different choice. I could also acknowledge the truth of my past experience. Time and again, when I feared I wouldn't measure up, I had risen to the challenge and succeeded.

I met head-on the irrational belief that had caused me to abandon music for hard work decades earlier. By their modeling, my parents created a strong work ethic in me, and I subconsciously linked my self-worth to career accomplishment. I also saw them doing more for others than for themselves. Yet, I recall my dad saying shortly before his sudden death, "You know, I regret I never learned how to play the piano." Through this musical journey, I had the chance to rediscover a long-lost part of me, to make amends with that teenager inside me who always wanted to jam with a band. I learned that if I wanted to avoid regret, I also needed to pay attention to doing what makes my heart sing. And how priceless was it when my then five-year-old son looked up at me from his lunchtime sandwich and asked, "Dad, when you grow up, are you going to be a musician?"

Whether I was *good enough* wasn't the question. Whether I *needed more time* to get good enough wasn't the question. Did I have the discipline to do what I love, regardless of how good I am—and did I have the patience to improve? *Those* were the real questions. The lesson embedded in this challenge transcended my musical journey to apply to my journey in life. I needed to let go of the belief that I wasn't good enough, pursue what I love and consciously create my desired future.

These lessons brought me to *Siddhartha Principle Three:* **CLARIFY. Create an Ideal Scene of your desired experience.** Visualize the end point the way you'd like it to look, feel, and be.

Great athletes have long used visualization techniques to spur spectacular performances. Olympic runners visualize themselves crossing the finish line with a world record time flashing on the scoreboard. Having learned from these peak performers in athletics, I applied their techniques when I was a gymnast in college. I was a specialist on the high bar, and this was typically the last of the six events. After warming up, I often had three hours to sit and watch the other performers. During this time, one option was to worry about my upcoming performance, seeing myself plunge to the ground in defeat. Instead, I spent that time visualizing an excellent outcome, seeing myself flawlessly executing every move in my routine. I even felt each subtle muscle movement in my body as I visualized my way through the performance.

Recalling what worked well in college, I marshaled a similar technique, taking this approach one step further. I developed an Ideal Scene for literally every song in the set list, both visualizing and writing down a clear and specific description of my future performance at The Cavern Club as if it was happening in the present tense.

I began by imagining in lush detail exactly what I'd see, feel, and do if my future unfolded in an ideal way. I designed the scene with a clear awareness of my capabilities, assuming I would be operating at my very best and most proficient, but not being totally unrealistic about my performance (I wouldn't have the bass lines of Paul McCartney nor the voice of John Lennon nor the moves of Mick Jagger!). I was willing to stretch beyond my typical limits of imagination, to be open to an outcome even better than what I could imagine.

I developed an Ideal Scene for every song in the performance as well as for my daily practices:

> *I'm attentively anticipating the bridges and solos, smoothly transitioning from one section to the next, as each finger confidently finds its string and note.*

I am easily creating plentiful time to immerse myself in my music, and calmly accepting perceived interruptions and setbacks to my practice schedule.

But to make this scene a reality, I thought I needed to spend one to four hours a day practicing. Where would that time come from? I was already busy with the rest of my life.

This required paying attention to *Siddhartha Principle Four*: **ACT. Take small steps every day to create your desired experience.** That meant aligning my daily planner with my true priorities (my desired experiences), because the way I spend my day is the way I spend my life. If I'm too busy to do what's truly important to me today, it's more likely I'll die with regrets when I run out of tomorrows.

Once we establish our priorities, it's essential to stay focused on them every day. The process begins by examining all the things we inadvertently say "Yes" to, whether out of obligation or from habit, and all the places we might be wasting time. Then we need to say NO to what's not a priority and a resounding YES to specific actions we can take each day that move us forward in reaching these essential goals. Because it was overwhelming to practice four hours every day, I just chose one small commitment that kept me moving forward, like practicing every day for 15 minutes. Often, starting with that intention led to longer sessions simply because I was enjoying it.

Months passed, and Stacey couldn't hit a few crucial high notes or sing all the harmonies on pitch, despite long hours with three singing coaches. Then she tried *Siddhartha Principle One*, singing a lower note that *was* in her range, and *Siddhartha Principle Four*, practicing the harmonies again and again every day. She would wake up in the middle of the night wondering if she was crazy being the lead singer in a rock band, but her perseverance amazed me, and so did her progress.

Meanwhile, I was wondering how in the world I would write an original song. I'd never written a song, and sharing my attempts at creativity required me to be vulnerable. I risked criticism. I had to push past my own self-doubts. In order to move forward, I eventually relied on a variation of *Siddhartha Principle One*: **What others think of you is none of your business**. And in fact, what *you* think about *yourself* in your limiting beliefs and negative thoughts is none of your business, either. You just need to meet yourself where you are, without judgment.

I started with small steps. I began toying with a variation of a bass line from another song, then, a melody finally emerged. For the lyrics, I decided to write about Stacey's emergence as a rock singer. I recalled the opening line from a Beatles song, "Drive My Car," beginning, "Asked a girl what she wanted to be," and I adapted it:

> *Asked myself what I wanted to be.*
> *I said, honey, there's more to see.*
> *I'm a mother, I'm a lover.*
> *Who am I undercover?*
> *I'm a rock star in my dreams.*

To finalize our preparations for our Cavern Club performance, our band played at a house party for 100 guests, then again at a local music club, which gave us exactly two public practice performances before our debut.

We did well, but all I could think of were the times I screwed up. Then my bass teacher, who had witnessed the performance, took me aside.

"Don," he confided, "you were great. You were solid. You were the glue that held the band together."

He gave me a valuable insight into controlling my own negative self talk. He also helped me discover a corollary to the first four *Siddhartha Principles*: **Achieving perfection can be redefined from never making a mistake to experiencing joy even when you do make mistakes.** On the eve of our departure for England, I felt an astonishing calm. Though we originally thought of Abbey Road and The Cavern Club as our destination, I realized that the inner journey in discovering and applying the *Siddhartha Principles* had been as valuable as the outer journey. No matter what, no one could take from me what I'd learned about myself.

And then came in one week the most intense living I'd experienced in a lifetime. We filmed part of a music video on the London Eye Ferris wheel and in a park across from the Houses of Parliament, Big Ben, and Westminster Abbey. We spent 14 hours at Abbey Road Studios, recording our song "One Ride," track by track. What a thrill to tap the keys of the piano, still in Studio 2, used to record the Beatles' "Ob-La-Di, Ob-La-Da" and play the final long chord of "A Day in the Life." Waiting after midnight for the final mix, Stacey and I lay on the floor of the studio in the dim light, gazing at the ceiling and allowing in the reality that *we really did just spend the day at Abbey Road recording our original song!*

We gave a hot, rocking performance at The Cavern Club, to the cheers of a real crowd (who were not already our friends). We spent our days there on a natural high, with fans stopping us in the street to tell Stacey, "Hey, I heard you at The Cavern Club. You sounded great!" The night after our performance, we were treated to a two-hour Paul McCartney concert in front of his home crowd in Liverpool's Anfield Stadium. The next night, we played our set to a packed house at the Cavern Pub, sister club to The Cavern, and were invited as guests of owner Bill Heckle to hear a private, backroom performance by former Wings guitarist Denny Laine.

Rory Best, brother of the Beatles' original drummer Pete, showed us around the Casbah, the coffee club in the basement of the Best family home, where the Beatles played in their early days. We had a long lunch with John Lennon's sister, Julia, and when she kissed us goodbye, Stacey laughed, "Wow! That was one degree of separation from kissing John Lennon." Our final night found us having an impromptu performance in the basement of The Jacaranda, another early Beatles haunt, where Stacey brought the house down with her belting rendition of "I'm Down."

Short on sleep, long on memories, I reached the end of the week astounded at what had come to me by simply leaning into something I loved, something that felt risky. I'd then discovered and used the *Siddhartha Principles* to bring it to fruition. I learned from the short journey to The Cavern Club that all I really have to do is listen for the song in my heart, and follow it.

In retrospect—looking back over the entire course of the project—I can see how it all evolved perfectly for my learning, growth and upliftment. The worry served a purpose to motivate me; facing the challenges helped me learn more about myself. Each step brought me to a better place. From that perspective arose the fifth Siddhartha Principle, to trust the process.

I recognized now that all my goals in life have simply been in service to my opportunity to learn new lessons. The *Siddhartha Principles* crystallized by working on a specific project; however, they also apply well to the rest of life. They truly help us make a conscious choice between living like a Salmon, or living like Siddhartha.

So, to summarize the *Siddhartha Principles*:

Siddhartha Principle One: **ACCEPT. Meet yourself where you are, without judgment.**

Siddhartha Principle Two: **LEARN. Find the lesson in your present challenge.**

Siddhartha Principle Three: **CLARIFY. Create an Ideal Scene of your desired experience.**

Siddhartha Principle Four: **ACT. Take small steps every day to create your desired experience.**

Siddhartha Principle Five: **TRUST. Have faith that your life is unfolding perfectly.**

Chapter 11: Happy to Be

*I wrote the song 'Happy to Be' based on phrases Don uses
regularly. It's like hearing his life philosophy in four minutes. It
captures what we've learned—and what we don't want to forget.*

—Stacey Fergusson, songwriter

On a plane over the Atlantic, I thought, *This may be the dumbest thing
I've ever done.* We were headed to the Highlands of Scotland to film
our first music video, *Silver Girl,* for our new band, Vanaka. We had a
storyboard and a two-person film crew, however, we still needed to
secure drums and lighting equipment, and find a cottage, a boat, a
meadow, a stand-in fiddle player, and a barn for the band scenes. We
needed permission from the local municipality to shoot on the Isle
of Skye. And oh yes, we needed the unpredictable Scottish weather
to cooperate for our three days of filming—not too much rain,
not too much sunshine, especially on the one day we hired the
helicopter. A crazy undertaking just to answer the question, "So,
what do you *do?*"

Back at home, over the last year, our band The Ride had gone
dormant. The Main Stage Dream Tours bandmates who had launched
us on the journey to Abbey Road and The Cavern Club returned
their focus to their own band. Stacey took up bass guitar herself, and
joined an all-girl band, Midnight Mynx. She now rehearsed with
her bandmates twice weekly as they developed an impressive set list
of cover songs, and the band landed local gigs. For shows around
Halloween, they wore sexy policewoman costumes and big smiles.
I felt uncomfortable with the attention they were getting, especially
from ogling men. Though my rational mind knew Stacey wasn't
going to run off with someone after a gig, I still felt threatened. And
I admit, I was jealous of her having so much fun. I thought, *Hey, what*

about my band?! And I resented my shift from bandmate to roadie and lead groupie.

By now, I'd learned to listen to my upset as a subconscious message that "School is in Session." Most likely, the surface issue probably wasn't the real issue. My fears of abandonment or feelings of jealousy had deeper roots.

Around this time, Stacey wrote and recorded a demo version of a song for me called "Anything." Her lyrics underscored the call to action:

> *I'll swim the seven seas*
> *I'll stand beside you when you dance with your ghosts*
> *And haunt your fantasies.*
> *Never question who loves you the most.*
> *I'll keep your heart safe in mine*
> *Through life's detours.*
> *I can't make you happy*
> *That choice is yours.*
> *I won't do everything for you*
> *But I'll do anything.*

I had to take personal responsibility for my own happiness. Time for *Siddhartha Principle One:* **ACCEPT. Meet yourself where you are, without judgment.**

I needed to get out of victim mode, quit blaming my wife, and reclaim my focus. That would involve redefining my own purpose and direction instead of feeling like Stacey's protector, roadie, and groupie. I'd learned that the first step when facing any challenging situation or turning point is to ask myself, "What qualities do I need to bring forward?" Just as in that meditation when I discovered "forgiveness" in the treasure chest, I needed to let my inner voice speak, and allow the answer to bubble up from my subconscious. I soon realized that after spending the past several years immersed in self-reflection, creativity, and intuition, I needed to step into leadership, self-empowerment, and accomplishment.

As we approached a milestone birthday for Stacey, she made a request that, serendipitously, provided the means for this next stage of my life and learning. Instead of taking a special trip or having a big party, she asked if we might celebrate by cutting an album. Since attending USM, Stacey had followed a lifelong dream, writing lyrics for more than twenty original songs. But as novice musicians ourselves, we needed help to produce an album. Just like the beginning of The Ride, we consulted with Jon Payne.

Besides being a close friend, extraordinary guitarist, and versatile singer, Jon tapped into an amazing community of local musicians. The idea of doing an album excited him. Stacey, Jon and I would become founders and core members of a new band, and we'd collaborate with others to develop and produce the songs.

In "meeting ourselves where we were, without judgment," Stacey and I would need to lose the self-defeating mindset that we couldn't do this just because we weren't lifelong professional musicians—or that we had to do it all ourselves. We recognized that the "Goal Road" of producing an album would really serve more as a "Learning Ladder" for our own personal growth and life experience. And I embraced this process as a means of discovering insights into my personal "entelechy."

The word entelechy dates back to Aristotle, who combined words meaning "complete or full-grown" with "being in motion towards becoming what one is." In modern terms, entelechy means realizing one's potential, being in the flow of the vital force that directs us toward self-fulfillment. From a larger perspective, it's our life purpose—an answer to my question, *So what do you do?*

We didn't know *how* we'd produce an album. We just knew that the *Siddhartha Principles* and other techniques we'd learned would serve us well in the process.

> Set my intention to capture the lesson
> And not know the answers, but live in the question.

> —Stacey Fergusson, "Happy to Be"

The next step was to consider *Siddhartha Principle Two:* **LEARN. Find the lesson in your present challenge.**

I intended to bring forward my leadership capabilities, my skills in getting things done, and my business acumen. And I also intended to utilize a different model than I'd originally used in business. Instead of setting stretch goals, having detailed action plans, and stressing out everyone to accomplish pre-determined objectives, what if this process could be more organic, more sensitive to the flow of events and opportunities, more about supporting others to shine? I could choose to remember that we're doing this for learning and for fun; not take ourselves too seriously; know that we always have the freedom to choose our response to any circumstance or opportunity; and have faith that whatever happens is in our highest good and the highest good of all concerned.

From my days at Rust-Oleum, I'd learned the importance of having allies—building a team of people who share my values, contribute unique talents, demonstrate loyalty and dedication, and take initiative to push beyond their comfort zones. I also had learned to take the Siddhartha approach rather than fighting my way upstream like a salmon. With clear *intention*, I need to pay attention to what floats my way. I can lean in to possibilities without having to *make* everything happen. If what I'm doing aligns with my purpose and the higher good, doors will open. I don't need to push for quick answers, but simply have the patience to *live in the question* until decisions become clear.

Some doors had already begun to open in the direction of building our team. For a live performance of The Ride's setlist at the Santa Barbara Harbor Festival, we needed a drummer and another singer. Jon asked the founders of a local band, Soul Majestic, to join us. Soon, Eric Iverson was keeping the beat and co-writing music for several of Stacey's songs. His wife, Oriana Sanders, brought her songbird voice to two lead vocals and harmonies on other tracks.

Meanwhile, Stacey began taking singing lessons from J.R. Richards. J.R., former lead singer and songwriter for the band Dishwalla, famous for his #1 Billboard hit "Counting Blue Cars," had moved on from the band, teaching singing lessons and producing other musicians. A multi-instrumentalist, brilliant songwriter, and phenomenal singer, he also had command of the technical aspects of recording, mixing, and editing. Stacey began working with him on her first song, "For A Good Time." In just two hours, J.R. cut a demo for the song. We asked if he'd produce our album, and he agreed.

Before long, we added more talent to the team. Jon Payne's friend, John Whoolilurie, a multi-instrumentalist who has played with Jack Johnson, ALO, and Les Claypool, added brilliant sax to our songs and filled in on anything else we needed, bringing a big heart to go with his nearly 7-foot tall frame. J.R.'s wife and business partner, Min Reid, stepped in to direct our photo and video shoots. Min was well qualified as a professional photographer and her skills as a brilliant (and now award-winning) director soon became evident. As the songs materialized over several months, J.R. introduced us to Brian Scheuble, recording and mixing engineer with credits including Elton John, Sheryl Crow, John Mayer, Ringo Starr, and U2's *Rattle and Hum* album.

In four days of sessions in our newly-upgraded home studio, the band recorded multiple takes of 10 tracks. Just the beginning. But we were on our way...to wherever we were going.

> *Choosing to be with those who help with my being*
> *Glad to say that I'm not a human doing*
> *You might call me lucky but I know what that luck is*
> *Knowing to look and to see where my friend lives.*
>
> —Stacey Fergusson, "Happy to Be"

As I had experienced during The Ride's build up to Abbey Road and The Cavern Club, I felt pressure to be as good as the rest of our band members. That spurred me to consistently take small steps to become fluent with the bass lines, practice the tricky fingering over and over, and continue my vocal practice.

As we launched into the production phase, the time came to more consciously employ *Siddhartha Principle Three:* **CLARIFY. Create an Ideal Scene of your desired experience.**

With the new team came a new band name: Vanaka ("vuh-NAH-kuh"), based on a combination of *vinaka,* a Fijian word translated as "thank you," and the Hindu *Vanakkam,* meaning "I bow to the divine in you," acknowledging the life force and Oneness within us all. Vanaka would stand for Divine Gratitude—the overall "desired experience" we intended to create through our music. The new album would be called, appropriately enough, *Gratitude.* A Vanaka logo emerged: an emblem based on an ancient Maori twist symbol that represents shared growth, community and wisdom; with a snake motif symbolizing reinvention; and an orange color that's associated with vitality.

J.R., Min, Stacey and I co-created an Ideal Scene for the Vanaka experience, envisioning the end result of what we'd create, as if it had already happened; and capturing our vision of how the process would flow, with joy, grace and ease. However, the most extraordinary Ideal Scene came as we prepared to shoot the music video *Silver Girl.*

Stacey wrote the song for our dear friend, Hollye Jacobs, who at 39 had been diagnosed with breast cancer. During the course of her treatment and subsequent recovery, she started a blog called *The Silver Pen* and then wrote a best-selling book, *The Silver Lining: A Supportive and Insightful Guide to Breast Cancer.* Hollye inspired Stacey with her courage, positive approach, and powerful life lessons. Song lyrics emerged, J.R. formulated the music and arrangement, and Oriana—a cancer survivor herself—stepped forward to lend her voice and authentic emotion to the lead vocal.

Not long after the song was recorded, I had a vision of filming the *Silver Girl* music video on the Cliffs of Moher, that rise 400 feet from the ocean along the west coast of Ireland. The location would honor Hollye's family name "Harrington" and underscore the immensity of her journey. But after "leaning in" to the idea, logistics and other complications ruled it out. Instead, we found a location that not only served Hollye's Gaelic heritage, but my family history as well: The Highlands of Scotland.

My first vision was to simply arrive in Scotland with a handheld video camera and film the band somewhere on location. Great plan! But as we involved Min and J.R., the vision soon expanded— and serendipity took over. Min created a storyboard and began scouting locations on the Internet, identifying the Isle of Skye for its spectacular scenery. J.R. and Min had gotten married earlier in the year at Eilean Donan castle, a 13th century stronghold destroyed in battle in 1719, then reconstructed. Situated on a small tidal island where three lochs meet, the castle would provide the perfect backdrop for some of the scenes. While contacting a video company in L.A. about shooting a wedding, Min discovered that one of the owners was a former rock star, a contemporary and friend of J.R. Given that connection, they agreed to do the shoot in Scotland, at an affordable price. Jon Payne asked his uncle in the U.K. whether he had any contacts in the Highlands that might help us. Amazingly, he did—a former colleague who now lived near Eilean Donan castle, with connections to others who could help us organize whatever we needed. Hollye and her husband Jeff accepted our invitation to join us in Scotland. But since our filming in the Isle of Skye would be two hours drive through the hills from our base camp outside of Inverness—and I couldn't find a suitable hotel on location—I thought of chartering a helicopter to transport them. When I looked for one online, I found a company that specialized in aerial filming—they'd shot scenes for the Harry Potter movies and Scottish promotional videos—located at Inverness airport, ten minutes from home base. As it turned out, I didn't use them for transportation, but hired the chopper for a day to shoot footage for the music video. Incredibly, doors were opening, and plans materializing.

Before leaving for Scotland, Stacey and I sketched an Ideal Scene on flipchart paper. In part, it read *"We are…*

Joyfully receiving gifts of serendipity.

Traveling with grace & timeliness as we safely arrive at our destinations.

Easily & gracefully assessing locations for the project.

Marveling at Nature's perfect timing in support of our filming & travels.

Gratefully acknowledging and accepting the "silver linings" of each situation.

Easily collaborating to refine & fulfill our creative vision.

Admiring our team's talent, wit, preparedness & resourcefulness.

Thankful for each team member's creative contributions & commitment.

Delightfully discovering the magic of Scotland's land & people.

Marveling at the spectacular, inspiring & far-reaching videos we co-create."

We'd prepared as best we could before leaving for Scotland, but so much was undone. We had to rely on our clear intentions, pay attention to the opportunities that presented themselves—and hope for serendipity—for everything to fall into place.

On our first night in the Highlands, Min, J.R., Stacey and I stayed at a tiny, remote hotel a 45-minute drive through the hills down a narrow one-lane road from Eilean Donan castle. We couldn't find another, better alternative. That night after dinner, we hoisted ale in the hotel's quaint little pub, and soon a duo began playing lively, traditional Scottish folk music—with guitar and a fiddle. After the show, the fiddle player agreed to join us for the video! The next morning, the owners of the hotel directed us a mile down the road to a friend's farm, with a barn we could use to film the band. Our contacts near Eilean Donan castle came up with a boat and the meadow, along with a rustic cottage on an island, owned by an elderly woman who visited now and then for solitude. Min gained permission to film around the famous Old Man of Storr, a set of rock pinnacles and grassy knolls along the coastline of the Isle of Skye.

Eric and Oriana spent a chilly, rainy day in the stone cottage on the island for the opening scenes. Dark clouds and rain came when we needed it. And as if on cue, at 10:30 p.m. as the summer sun set behind the distant mountains, and Oriana perched on a craggy rock at the water's edge singing, "Know the sun shines out on the other side, gently lift up the cloud's veil, and we find life's silver lines," the clouds parted and brilliant rays backlit her figure, as the wind lifted her velvet cape. The cameramen looked at each other in amazement and exclaimed, "Can you believe that just happened?"

The next morning at the Isle of Skye, the coastal wind gusted to gale force. The helicopter company said it was up to the pilot whether he would fly and film in those conditions. It was our one and only day to make it happen. The pilot, a cigarette-smoking Russian, was game for the challenge. After dropping Oriana on a narrow bluff above the sea, the helicopter circled low over the water, screaming back towards the cliffs for a spectacular rising shot. As the chopper circled overhead, Oriana let loose from her hand the metaphoric silver ribbon—just as the wind stopped dead, and the ribbon fell to her feet! On the second take, the wind cooperated and the ribbon blew off the hilltop, cascading down the bluff to the sea, with Min in the back of the helicopter shouting at the pilot, "Don't lose that ribbon! Stay on that ribbon!" The scene still gives me goosebumps every time I see it.

Our last day of filming met with constant drizzle, the only day that it couldn't affect us: we shot scenes of the band in the barn, playing "Silver Girl," complete with our stand-in fiddler. Yes, even the weather had cooperated with our Ideal Scene.

The *Silver Girl* music video stands as one of the finest examples of project management and teamwork I've ever experienced throughout my business career, and attests to the power of the Siddhartha Principles. We "met ourselves where we were" when we started the project, and assembled a team of highly talented and committed individuals. We all saw the learning opportunities present in our challenges, and approached each obstacle as an opportunity. Our Ideal Scene became a subconscious guide, as each person consciously took personal responsibility to execute their part of the project—and everyone stepped out of their comfort zone to tackle things they'd never done before. Each individual rose to a new level of skill and confidence by taking small steps along the Goal Road, with the full support of everyone else on the team. In the end, we had to trust each other—and have faith that everything would come together beautifully, despite not being able to control every element. Most importantly, we created a most memorable life experience and deepened our friendships.

Enjoy the ride and reach for the goal line
Learning and laughing while we climb up the soul line.

—Stacey Fergusson, "Happy to Be"

What started naively as a three-month project, stretched into three years. *Siddhartha Principle Four* kept us focused: **ACT. Take small steps every day to create your desired experience.**

Rather than attempt to push through the over-dubbing and mixing process on an unrealistic and stressful timetable, we started booking two days at a time at NRG Studios in North Hollywood, spread out over several months, taking an average of one day per song. This gave our creativity space to breathe and invited serendipity to play along with us.

As we neared the completed mix of the song "For a Good Time," we recorded the track on CD and listened to it on the car stereo in the NRG parking lot. At 3:19 on the track, there's a single stroke drum roll from snare across the toms, and the idea came to me of having it start in the left speaker, slowly flow to center and then to the right speaker, a technique I'd heard on records by Jimi Hendrix and Led Zeppelin. I took the idea back inside to Brian and J.R. Brian's eyes lit up, "I've got another idea." Soon, he wheeled in two ancient reel-to-reel tape decks. "There's a technique where we can record the track onto both of these decks, start them together, and then slow one of them down by dragging a hand on the reel. They fight to keep up with each other, and produce a slightly out-of-phase effect that could sound really cool."

Great, I thought! Four hours later, J.R. and Brian had nearly given up. This wasn't a computer-controlled digital process, but a manual one. Getting the timing just right proved nearly impossible. After taking a break, wherein I thought Brian had dumped the idea, he came back with renewed determination. "OK, one more try. I'm gonna do it this time!" And he did. The swirling effect remains a highlight of the song, and as if making a final statement, like a triumphant fist in the air, Brian ended the mix with an extended last note that radiates into space as the song fades out.

We also took our time, in a series of small steps, for the songs "Still Beautiful" and "Anything." Two and a half years into the project, we had 10 of 12 songs completed. The lyrics for "Still Beautiful" and "Anything" had long since been written, but the musical arrangements just weren't coming together. I felt some internal pressure to make a dash for the goal line. With 10 songs, we had a quorum for the album. Sharing that opinion with J.R. and Stacey prompted renewed action.

Before long, J.R. had cut a gorgeous demo of "Still Beautiful"— and asked if he might sing the guest lead vocal on the song (just as Stacey and I were about to ask him!). The song held a special place in our hearts, as Stacey had written it after the Sandy Hook Elementary School shooting of 2012. In response to our young son asking why such a tragic event had happened—and his words "I feel hollow inside"—Stacey's lyrics provide inspiration to continue to look for the goodness in mankind and "let love lead." Subsequently, we filmed the music video at the historic Granada Theatre in Santa Barbara, interpreting the song through dance—and even calling in a Scottish piper we'd met during the filming of *Silver Girl*. Sandy Hook has since utilized our video to garner support for their work, and adopted the line, "Let Love Lead." Looking back, we can't imagine our album without such a rich song, which evolved from taking one step at a time towards a greater vision.

Similarly, the song "Anything" came together when I set a soft deadline, and gave J.R. and Jon the freedom to develop the musical arrangement. The crowning jewel appeared when our friend Luis Conte joined us at NRG Studios and overdubbed percussion, both on that song and "The Sweet Spot." Just off a tour with James Taylor and in between gigs as a composer and percussionist on *Dancing with the Stars*, Luis pulled from his three tall crates of eclectic instruments gathered from around the world, adding a deep richness to the tracks.

Staying present where I'm on the planet
And not taking anything I have for granted.

—Stacey Fergusson, "Happy to Be"

The Vanaka project exemplifies all the *Siddhartha Principles*, none more than *Siddhartha Principle Five:* **TRUST. Have faith that your life is unfolding perfectly.** Interestingly, the completion and launch of the album and videos brought up an old belief system I've had around fear of success. I feared being drawn deep into business (or busy-ness), and upsetting my life balance. I'd run up against these issues before with previous ventures. As I dug deeper into the pattern, I recognized that the roots dated back to my experience at Rust-Oleum. That career had consumed me with constant stress and time pressures. I had held the belief that it in some way contributed to the breakdown of my marriage and my divorce war. If I associated such pain with success, no wonder I hesitated launching Vanaka into the public realm! It's easy to play small with the illusion that it will keep us safe.

In retrospect, my success at Rust-Oleum provided the freedom I have today. The stress I experienced back then came from a lack of self-awareness and life skills, not from the work itself. My divorce derived from incompatibility and not knowing how to create an intimate relationship, not because of my busy-ness. The two-and-a-half year divorce that I'd held as my most painful period actually brought the biggest gifts—for my learning and growth—paving the way for the life and relationships I have today. My previous foundations had to be destroyed to usher in a different way of being.

One morning, I meditated to gain confidence in my next steps. Into the silence, I took the question, "In what ways am I keeping myself small?" After a few moments, I had the sensation of rising higher, and an image appeared, as if above my head: a Spiritual Master holding me in his arms. He said, "*The Siddhartha metaphor didn't come to you by accident. Live that model of life.*" Then I became a ball of light, radiating out in all directions. I had the sensation that I was love, coming from love. The lyrics of "Happy to Be" came to mind: *Every day in every way, all my love is shining*. I had a vision, seeing myself from behind facing a cheering audience in a huge venue, blinding stage lights "backlighting" my figure. I had no fear, no ego. I just radiated gratitude for being able to touch and uplift this audience with our words and music.

The *Siddhartha* story is the "hero's journey"—how wisdom evolves from the crucible of experience, and we recognize the perfection in the flow of life. The peace I gained from the meditation came as I detached from end results and trusted that whatever evolves will be for the highest good. I could simultaneously invite myself to live in the question, "How does it get better than this?" and know the real answer is, "It just does!" I discovered that for me, "entelechy" isn't a question of *what to do*, but *how to be*—and how I can positively impact others. What I do simply arises from my authentic way of being.

I've no regrets for back then, and no fear for maybe when.
I meet myself where I am, 'cause it's the best place I've ever been.

—Stacey Fergusson, "Happy to Be"

Chapter 12: Some Kind of Wonderful

In this hour, Siddhartha ceased to fight with his destiny, ceased to suffer. On his face blossomed the serenity of a knowledge that was no longer opposed by will, a knowledge that knew perfection, that consented to the flow of events, with the stream of life, full of compassion, full of shared delight, surrendered to the stream, belonging to the unity of all things.

I closed my eyes, then began to imagine my life as a blank slate, trying to let go of everything that defined me. One by one, I erased everything. I started with my work, letting go of the emails waiting for me, scheduled events and meetings, my "to do" list, and my plans. I imagine my life with no financial concerns. Forget that the stock market exists, let go of tracking my accounts, release the fear that I won't have enough. I imagine I have no money; money doesn't even exist. I let go of my house and all my possessions.

I let go of any health concerns. I release my attachments to my wife, ex-wife, friends, family, community, people I resented or fought with, my memories, and my expectations. I erase time—it's imaginary anyway. I erase my values and my goal to be wise, creative, wealthy, punctual, and nice. I release all goals for my lifetime. I let go of my spiritual beliefs. Then, finally, I imagine I have no body, no emotions.

After all, eventually we die and lose everything. Having let go of all the things that had defined me up until now, from this place of nothingness, without any restrictions or obligations, I ask myself, *Who am I?*

After a few moments, an unexpected thought bubbles up: *You are a spiritual learner and teacher.* Really? That idea seems completely overwhelming. I don't have God in my i-Phone Favorites. I've got no guru and don't spend my days praying. Don't I need to be *Enlightened* with a capital E? Or at least know how to levitate? Or is it really like Father Guido Sarducci said on *Saturday Night Live*, that these days anybody can be a saint, even if most of our miracles are just card tricks?

The following day, I shared with my Young Presidents Organization forum group what had surfaced in my meditation. They insisted, "You're already a spiritual learner and teacher! You have a master's degree in spiritual psychology, you run almost every one of our retreats, and you've taught us how to create Ideal Scenes and use the power of our subconscious minds."

"Well, thanks," I murmured, a bit taken aback. "But…I don't *feel* like a spiritual learner and teacher. Coach, facilitator, mentor—that may be. But when it comes to 'spiritual psychology,' I think I've focused more on the psychology part. I don't really feel comfortable embracing my own spirituality."

Reflecting on this conversation during my drive home, I remembered my coach Jonathan suggesting that there's a spectrum of teachers. On one side, the facilitator or coach. On the other, those like the Dalai Lama. They may use similar tools, but the spiritual teacher also embodies a different quality. The further one shifts towards the spiritual side of the spectrum, the less heaviness—the more joy. The spiritual teacher walks with extraordinary lightness, and by creating a gentle and uplifting environment, invites spiritual learners to experience a deeper self-awareness and transformation.

I recognized that I still identified more with the role of facilitator and coach, and needed to explore how to move towards the spiritual end of the spectrum. When I got home, I decided to continue my meditation from the day before. I closed my eyes, settled into a relaxed state, and asked myself, "What qualities do I need to bring forward to move towards the role of spiritual learner and teacher?" After a few moments of listening in silence, three qualities emerged from my subconscious: Confidence, Enthusiasm, and Faith. Interestingly, each quality related to Spirit. The root of *confidence* means "having trust in someone or something." *Enthusiasm* comes from the Greek *entheos*, which means "the god within." And *faith* means trust in oneself and in Spirit.

For much of my life, laboring under the weight of obligation had kept me busy moving the stones of "doing" rather than experiencing the spontaneity of feeling and just "being." The more time I spent moving stones, the more I believed I was in control of my life. However, I'd come to realize that control is an illusion. There are always circumstances we can't foresee; and even those we do see are rarely under our control. The more we try to control, the less we surrender to faith.

In my mind's eye, I now stepped past the old stones of doing. Beyond the stones lay the vast nothingness of the Universe. What would it be like to walk into that void, into faith?

I was reminded of the scene in *Indiana Jones and the Last Crusade*, when Indiana Jones, making his way through a narrow tunnel, arrives at an impassable chasm. The path continues on the other side, but the chasm's too wide to jump. At first panicked, but finally, with faith, he steps out into the gap—and a bridge appears, allowing him to cross to the other side.

As I looked back at the chasms that appeared in my life—like the challenges of Rust-Oleum and my divorce—my response had been to try to ignore my problems, control the outcome, or escape. By judging that the challenges were bad or wrong, I had often reacted with panic, anger or denial. That limited my choices, and made me less effective. The reality is that all the challenges of my life have been for my learning. They are actually gifts. And the biggest gift of them all is to realize that the invisible bridge of faith has been there all along. Stepping onto that bridge allows me to stay calm in the face of challenges, seek the learning opportunities in difficult situations, and find more creative solutions. In faith, I discover greater confidence and enthusiasm for my life.

The first four *Siddhartha Principles* allow us to meet challenges in a more peaceful way, clearly visualize what we want to create, and take action towards our goals. When we meet ourselves where we are, without judgment, we can approach our challenges from a place of greater clarity and creativity. We take dominion over our situation and make conscious choices. When we adopt the perspective that every challenge, obstacle, or painful situation is a learning opportunity, we begin looking for the blessings instead of wallowing in victimhood. We go deep inside and connect with our courage. We ask, "How can I use this situation to become wiser, and to be unconditionally loving of myself and others?" From this place of empowerment, we can visualize an Ideal Scene for what we want to create. We can focus on the positive, giving ourselves some room to breathe and permission to dream. We then feel more confident in taking a small step towards our desired destination.

But what happens when despite all of our best efforts to employ these *Siddhartha Principles*, we still feel stuck, still struggle, still hurt? That's where faith comes in. Faith is our acceptance that our current circumstances serve some higher purpose; faith is also a positive assumption about the future. By definition, there's no logical proof or material evidence to support either the acceptance or the assumption. Given that we have clarified our goals and taken appropriate action, we then simply have a choice: struggle in negativity and despair, or settle into faith.

Acceptance means that we can choose to *believe* that there is a good reason why things are unfolding as they are, and that our challenging situations provide an opportunity to learn deep and important spiritual lessons from the obstacles that life places in our path. Rather than condemning what life has offered us, acceptance means that we authentically embrace it, even when it's the last thing we would have wished for ourselves. We're willing to see our situation as a gift, not a curse.

Once we accept our circumstances, faith offers a solid bridge to the future. Like Indiana Jones, we need to step into the chasm, having done the best we can, and trust that an unseen alternative will appear at the right time. We simply assume that the future holds a positive outcome. The more I trust and have faith that this is the way the Universe works, the more peaceful I feel, the more gratitude I have for the blessings of each day, and the less I worry about the future or things I can't control. If I'd known how good life was going to turn out downstream, I wouldn't have fought so hard against the current.

The most important lesson of my life is *Siddhartha Principle Five*: **TRUST. Have faith that your life is unfolding perfectly.**

～

One sunny afternoon, I sailed the Santa Barbara Channel with some friends. As a 15-knot breeze filled the sails, I told my friends that I was writing a book outlining an approach to life, the *Siddhartha Principles*. One of them asked, "If you hadn't sold your company, made a lot of money, and quit your job as president, could you still operate like Siddhartha rather than a Salmon?"

A good question. But let's unwind the assumptions. First of all, it presupposes that once someone makes a lot of money, they're happy and set for life. Research tells us, though, that people who win millions in the lottery, after one year, don't find themselves any happier than they were before they won all the money. They have a "set point" of happiness they haven't learned to change. The honest truth is my own set point didn't shift following the sale of my company, until I took action to shift it. I also recall the story of an executive who made a fortune when his Internet company went public, and not long afterward decided to step in front of a train. All that money couldn't overcome his personal demons. My fundamental work, and the work of all of us, involves shifting the happiness set point, not chasing money.

On the flipside, my friend's question contained a built-in assumption that people without financial resources are excluded from joy. Is it really true that without money, we can't be happy? Of course not! Of the seven billion people on the planet, most don't live in affluence. People find their happiness in their families, their community, their work, their play. A person may walk 10 miles to the river for water and still carry a smile in their heart. Happiness depends not on a person's abundant resources but on their response to life's challenges and their capacity to experience gratitude and contribute to the lives of others.

Certainly, there may be truth in what a successful entrepreneur friend once told me: "I've been rich, I've been poor. Rich is better." Poverty presents many challenges, and has led to great suffering. I have little knowledge and no personal experience of poverty. Wealth absolutely provides both the opportunity to meet all our basic needs and many more options. But wealth doesn't guarantee happiness. In fact, sometimes having material success can lull someone into thinking they don't have to do their inner work. No matter our circumstances, we all have work to do if we wish to experience happiness.

This holds true even if someone has retired, as they do not automatically shift into bliss mode. I've shared my own challenges in redefining myself after selling the company, trying to answer the question, "So, what do you *do*?" I've observed many people experiencing misery or depression after selling their business or retiring. Their sense of purpose was defined solely by what they did. They had never taken the time to discover who they really are. I once received a call from a friend who had recently sold his business, made enough money to be set for life, but was now distraught about how to fill his time. He confided that his father had always judged success solely by the title shown on someone's business card. Driven by his early conditioning, and with nothing to "do," he felt his life had lost meaning. He fell into a deep depression.

I wasn't depressed after selling my company, but I kept a full schedule, always wishing there were more hours in the day. Granted, I got to choose more of what I really wanted to do. But that didn't guarantee peace and happiness. As an example, I went trout fishing one Autumn, just myself and a guide. Here I am on a remote mountain stream, in pristine wilderness, not another fisherman within 20 miles, and plentiful world-class trout. Sun shining, blue sky above, I am surrounded by an extraordinary outer world. And what do I find myself doing in my inner world? Criticizing myself for blowing a cast, spooking a fish, tangling my line, losing the big one! What an amazing realization: My happiness depends not on what I'm doing, but by how I'm *being with myself* while I'm doing it.

There's yet another subtle side to the question about "not working" and its link to happiness. It goes like this: "Because I'm working full time, I'm too busy to be happy." On the contrary, operating like Siddhartha rather than a Salmon is not dependent on external circumstances. You can be extremely busy and happy, extremely busy but unhappy, or live a life of leisure filled with sadness—or joy. In all cases, embedding the *Siddhartha Principles* in our daily lives supports us in making internal choices that lead to greater peace, joy, and wisdom.

To review the principles:

Siddhartha Principle One: **ACCEPT. Meet yourself where you are, without judgment.** Express your emotions—your anger, sadness or fear—and examine what beliefs and patterns are fueling them. Identify the Should's that prevent you from accepting reality and suspend your beliefs about what's *Bad* and *Wrong*.

Once you reach a place of neutrality, use *Siddhartha Principle Two:* **LEARN. Find the lesson in your present challenge.** This principle helps you reframe your issues as learning opportunities. Ask yourself, "If my soul designed this situation to teach me something I need to learn or let go of, what might that be?" Accepting the lesson as a gift, no matter how painful, shifts you from griping to gratitude, from pessimism to positivity.

Positivity paves the way for *Siddhartha Principle Three:* **CLARIFY. Create an Ideal Scene of your desired experience.** This unleashes the powers of your creativity. Develop Ideal Scenes to establish new expectations and intentions for yourself. What is the life you really hope to create? Dream beyond your comfort zone while staying grounded in reality.

Once you've identified what you'd like to create, start moving in the direction of your dreams with *Siddhartha Principle Four:*

ACT. Take small steps to create your desired experience. Be prepared to accept what the Universe brings to you in return. Stay open to accomplishing your intended goal, or shifting direction to achieve something even better.

Sometimes things unfold in ways we wouldn't have predicted or couldn't imagine, and that's where the last principle comes in. Employ *Siddhartha Principle Five:* **TRUST. Have faith that your life is unfolding perfectly.** Trust that whatever is happening is exactly as it should be, for your learning, your growth, and your spiritual evolution.

Consistently following the *Siddhartha Principles* helps us navigate life's challenges with greater ease. We can accomplish many goals using either the Siddhartha or Salmon approach. The Salmon way is not "wrong," just more challenging because it's more painful. As I look back to the Salmon times of my life, they led me to where I needed to be, but I learned through pain. It's not realistic to assume we can go through life without obstacles, disappointment, hurt or loss. Wisdom comes as we learn from our experiences. Pain is simply part of the process. But eventually, as we learn our lessons, we can apply our knowledge, tempered by experience. With wisdom, we can arrive at our goals more elegantly, with less effort and more joy. Both Salmon and Siddhartha must take action to achieve their goals. The difference lies in their motivation and Way of Being. Fear pushes the Salmon. Love draws Siddhartha forward. Seriousness, control, and self-reliance become the *Salmon operandi*. Siddhartha trusts the process, collaborates, stays aware, and has faith. This way results in more lightness and a knowing smile.

The sculptor Michelangelo once said that in carving a statue, he simply freed the interior figure from everything that didn't belong to it. Like excess marble, many of the self-judgments that once imprisoned me have fallen away, and after a very long search, I've learned what to say when asked the question, "So what do you do?"

Now I answer: "As much as possible, I do what I love."

Slowly there blossomed, and slowly ripened within Siddhartha
the realization, the knowledge of what wisdom really was,
and what would be the goal of his long quest.
It was nothing more than a readiness of the soul, a capacity,
a secret art of thinking, feeling, breathing in, at every instant,
in the midst of life, the idea of unity. Slowly this blossomed
within him...harmony, knowledge of the eternal perfection of
the world, a smile, unity.

Gratitude

I acknowledge the essential contributions of my coach and dear friend, Jonathan Brennan, in the editing, development and production of this book—and am grateful for his extraordinary patience, encouragement, thoroughness, and insight. Thanks also to Norman Kolpas, who helped edit an early version of the book and mentored me as a writer. Huge gratitude to Irene Rietschel for her skillful book design, translation of Siddhartha quotes from the original German text, and for her cheerful patience throughout countless editorial changes. I appreciate the careful proofreading and editorial suggestions of my longtime friend Kimra Green, who added value to the final edition. Love and gratitude to Stacey, my True Companion, who continues to make living, learning and loving such a joy—and who suggested some important touches to the text.

Thanks, too, to my Masterminds, YPO forum group, USM friends, Rust-Oleum executives and others who read early versions of this book and provided valuable feedback. In particular, I'm indebted to Kevin MacDonald and Steve McDonald, who read each and every one of the many versions of this book, providing hugely important insights and encouragement along the way. I'm also grateful for the wise suggestions and helpful reflections of Jeff Jacobs, Bob Zollars, Robin Ferracone and Bill Kerr.

Deep gratitude to Andie Luce, who was a beacon in my darkest days. Heartfelt thanks to Jeff Green for a long-enduring friendship, and to Greg Willsey for being a longtime partner in personal growth and keeping my financial house in order, and to Adde and Mike Waters for friendship, collaboration, and course-corrective feedback at critical times in my life.

I am grateful to Mary and Ron Hulnick for the learning and experiences I acquired from the master's program in Spiritual Psychology at the University of Santa Monica. I also credit them with the concept of the "Goal Road" (Goal Line) and "Learning Ladder" (Learning/Soul Line) presented in the Introduction. For helping me discover the power of acceptance, forgiveness, compassion, and unconditional loving, I am indebted to the Hulnicks, the USM program, the faculty, my project team (the *Wild Majestics*), and my fellow students.

I am also grateful for Arleah & Morrie Shechtman, my mentors through divorce and the sale of Rust-Oleum, who taught me much about how to create and maintain intimate relationships. To my children, for their love and all I've learned from them. To the Captain, and to my dad, Donald W. Fergusson, who modeled integrity, modesty, perseverance, and dedication, and who provided me the opportunity to continue the legacy at Rust-Oleum. To my mom, Marjorie P. Fergusson, for her faith in me, her generosity, and her courage to move on.

Thanks to my sister Jeanne and my cousin Sue, who supported me through the travails of the Rust-Oleum sale. To Rex Reade and Bud Bartelt, my loyal mentors at Rust-Oleum. To all those with whom I worked at the company—whether supporting or challenging me—for the amazing education, growth, and prosperity they helped make possible.

My appreciation for the Riders and Vanakers, amazing musicians and collaborators who have contributed to the latest creative and joyful chapter of my life. Especially, I'm grateful to Jon Payne, a loyal friend who helps make my "Ideal Scenes" of music and sailing come to fruition.

Thanks also to the many people who supported me, challenged me, and came into my life at just the right moment throughout my journey, even if I didn't specifically mention them in this book.

Finally, my gratitude to Sally and Tim, who sent me on the greatest path of learning and personal growth imaginable. They, perhaps more than anyone, provided the impetus for me to make self-honoring choices—and discover the power of forgiveness.

The Siddhartha Principles

1. ACCEPT.

Meet yourself where you are, without judgment.

2. LEARN.

Find the lesson in your present challenge.

3. CLARIFY.

Create an Ideal Scene of your desired experience.

4. ACT.

Take small steps every day to create your
desired experience.

5. TRUST.

Have faith that your life is unfolding perfectly.